"Few people in this country know as much about community building as Jim Diers. The case studies and ideas in this book are extremely powerful evidence that real communities are knit together by the public places they share, and they show how small ideas from ordinary citizens can make an entire city thriving and beautiful."—**Fred Kent**, President, Project for Public Spaces

"Seattle's Department of Neighborhoods is widely known as the most innovative effort in the U.S. to empower local residents, and Diers captures the extensive array of strategies and programs devised by his department. This is a very readable account that touches on many of the major challenges facing every city in the country."—**John P. Kretzmann**, co-author of *Building Communities from Inside Out*

"Dozens of towns, cities, and suburbs are replicating the outstanding community-building programs pioneered by Seattle's Department of Neighborhoods. *Neighbor Power* supplies the inspiration and the techniques for building strong neighborhood communities from the ground up."—**Judy Corbett**, Executive Director, Local Government Commission

"Finally, a book sharing the 'how we did it' of Seattle's neighborhoods. *Neighbor Power* bursts with inspirational ideas, proven in practice, for building community. It is a must read for all students of planning and community development, local government managers and elected officials, and neighborhood leaders—in fact, anyone who cares about how we live together and create community."—**Linda Campbell**, Manager for City Council, Shellharbour, Australia

"Jim Diers's approach to neighborhood empowerment is gaining popularity in Japan. Thanks to *Neighbor Power*, we can now put Seattle's programs into action."—**Yuko Nishimura**, Komazawa University, Tokyo

Neighbor Power

BUILDING COMMUNITY
THE SEATTLE WAY

Neighbor Power

BUILDING COMMUNITY
THE SEATTLE WAY

JIM DIERS

UNIVERSITY OF WASHINGTON PRESS

Seattle and London

University of Washington Press
PO Box 50096, Seattle, WA 98145
www.washington.edu/uwpress

Library of Congress Cataloging-in-Publication Data
Diers, Jim.
Neighbor power : building community the Seattle way/
Jim Diers.—1st ed.
p. cm.
Includes bibliographical references and index.
ISBN 978-0-295-98444-5 (pbk. : alk. paper)
1. Community development—Washington
(State)—Seattle. I. Title.
HN80.S54D53 2004 307.1'4'09797772—dc22 2004013595

*Cover illustration (top): Miller Park residents celebrating completion of the
Ron K. Bills Fountain. Photo by Ian Edelstein; courtesy City of Seattle.*

The troll is as good a symbol as any of the remarkable neighborhood spirit in Seattle. It's really a tale about ways that our elected city governments can give power back to ordinary people. — ELIZABETH AIRD, columnist, *Vancouver Sun*

The Fremont Troll attracts people from all over the world, including these monks from Tibet's Monks of Ganden Shartse. Photograph by Gilbert W. Arias, © 2001, Seattle Post-Intelligencer; reprinted with permission.

CONTENTS

Acknowledgments   ix

Introduction   3

1 / VALUING COMMUNITY
The Department of Neighborhoods' Origins   18

2 / ORGANIZING COMMUNITIES
Involving All Neighbors and Other Programs   31

3 / CONNECTING COMMUNITIES
Neighborhood Service Centers and District Councils   44

4 / BUILDING COMMUNITY
The Neighborhood Matching Fund   55

5 / CULTIVATING COMMUNITY
The P-Patch Program   101

6 / SUSTAINING COMMUNITIES
The Neighborhood Planning Program   128

7 / CELEBRATING COMMUNITY
   Neighbor Appreciation Day 141

8 / MODELING COMMUNITY
   Columbia City 147

9 / REPLICATING NEIGHBORHOOD PROGRAMS 161

10 / CONCLUSION 168

   Appendix A
   Maps 176

   Appendix B
   Neighborhood Matching Fund Guidelines 179

   Bibliography 193

   Index 195

ACKNOWLEDGMENTS

My passion for community building comes from the generous support that I have received from the members of my own community. Without them, there would be no Department of Neighborhoods, and I certainly would not have written this book.

Thank you to the members of my workplace community, beginning with the elected officials under whom I served. Mayor Charles Royer, thank you for taking a big chance by hiring me and for insisting that neither the Office of Neighborhoods nor the district councils should become a layer of bureaucracy between the neighborhoods and city government. I am indebted to Mayor Norm Rice for reorganizing the office into a Department of Neighborhoods and retaining me as director; Norm, thank you for helping me understand the importance of Seattle's non-geographic communities and for embarking on the bold experiment in bottom-up planning. I am especially appreciative of Mayor Paul Schell, who understands that government's role should be to support community initiatives; thank you, Paul, for tripling the Neighborhood Matching Fund and for decentralizing city government so that it could follow up on the neighborhoods' plans. None of the mayors could have done anything without a supportive city council; all of the members deserve my gratitude; in particular, thank you to Jim Street, who is the true father of the Department of Neighborhoods, and to Richard Conlin, who followed Jim as the champion of the department and of Seattle's neighborhoods.

The credit for the success of the Department of Neighborhoods belongs to my co-workers. You are truly an amazing group of skilled and dedicated public servants. You walk the talk; every one of you is active in your own communities and, together, you created a richly diverse workplace community that continues to embrace and inspire me. I always felt fortunate to be part of such a wonderful team, but it was not until I was gone from the department that I realized just how dependent I had become. Fortunately, Laurie Dunlap, my administrative assistant, took pity on me and volunteered to do all the initial editing of my manuscript; thank you, Laurie, for your ongoing friendship, advice, and ability to make me seem more literate than I am.

Mayor Rice always said that I had the best job in the city, and he was right, because I had the rare pleasure of working with virtually every community in Seattle. I appreciate all of the community activists who welcomed me so warmly and taught me so patiently. I never ceased to be inspired by your deep commitment to the community and by your remarkable accomplishments. Everywhere I go in Seattle, I see evidence of your care for the city and for one another. Any credit that the Department of Neighborhoods has received really belongs to you.

Finally, thank you to my most immediate community—my family. Dorothy and Herman Diers, my parents, have always been my role models. My father has been a lifelong advocate for peace and justice. Through her words and actions, my mother taught me that it is as important to care for your own community as it is to care for the larger world. My parents raised a family of dynamic activists. Mom, Dad, Gary, Brent, Paul, and Judy, you make me so proud.

The love of my life is Sarah Driggs, my partner for the past thirty years, and our children, Kati and Joey. They have been consistently supportive of my work in spite of the many evening meetings and weekend events that it has entailed. Kati and Joey have developed their own richly diverse communities; they give me great hope for the future. Sarah has an amazing ability to make time for her family, career, and a vast array of other interests. She keeps me centered. While I have been talking community, Sarah is the one who has volunteered in our community's schools and Little League, and who knows all of our neighbors. She encouraged me to write this book and made it possible for me to do so. It is to you—Sarah, Kati, and Joey—that I dedicate this book.

Neighbor Power

BUILDING COMMUNITY
THE SEATTLE WAY

INTRODUCTION

Community building has been my preoccupation and my career for all twenty-eight years I have lived in Seattle, but I have made time for other activities—for instance, bowling. I have bowled with my family, my friends, and my co-workers, and I have bowled in fund-raisers for local community organizations. I have visited bowling alleys throughout Seattle's neighborhoods and from Cuernavaca to Tokyo.

So I was intrigued when Robert Putnam came out with a book titled *Bowling Alone*. Solitary bowling was a phenomenon I had never considered, much less experienced. I had to know why anyone would want to bowl *alone*.

I was relieved to learn that Putnam didn't really mean it—not literally. He was simply using shorthand to describe the dramatically declining participation in American bowling leagues. His research shows that even though more people were bowling in 1996 than ever before—91 million—the percentage of adults in bowling leagues plummeted from 6 percent in 1965 to 2 percent in 1996.

Putnam documents similar drops in membership numbers for a wide variety of other voluntary associations during that same period. His list includes the League of Women Voters, American Bar Association, NAACP, Red Cross, Elks, Shriners, Jaycees, Grange, PTAs, churches, political parties, and many more. Whereas in the 1960s nearly half of all Americans participated in clubs and local associations on a weekly basis, in the 1990s fewer than one-quarter did so.

Not only are Americans going to fewer meetings, claims Putnam, but they are also spending less time schmoozing with one another. The last third of the twentieth century saw a precipitous drop in the number of people who play cards and a similar drop in the number of people who send greeting cards. With the declining frequency of picnics, dinner parties, and family meals, and the shrinking patronage of neighborhood bars, today's Americans are also less likely to share food and drink.

So what do bars, bar associations, and bowling leagues have in common, and why should we care that fewer people are participating in them? Putnam says that all these declines are signs of the erosion of what he calls "social capital." Putnam defines social capital as "connections among individuals—social networks and norms of reciprocity and trustworthiness that arise from them." He concludes that "our growing social capital deficit threatens educational performance, safe neighborhoods, equitable tax collection, democratic responsiveness, everyday honesty, and even our health and happiness."

Eric Klinenberg documents the serious consequences that a social capital deficit had for the health of Chicago's North Lawndale neighborhood during the heat wave of 1995. North Lawndale is located adjacent to Little Village, a neighborhood with a similar proportion of low-income seniors living alone. That similarity notwithstanding, Little Village's busy streets and vibrant businesses fostered social connections, while North Lawndale's lack of commercial activity and high crime rate caused its residents to live in isolation. Klinenberg cites that isolation as the major reason why North Lawndale experienced a death rate ten times higher than Little Village's in the heat wave that claimed the lives of more than seven hundred Chicagoans.

Putnam also sees social capital as essential to the health of democracy. His statistics show social capital and democratic participation declining along parallel tracks. Between 1973 and 1993, the number of Americans working for a political party dropped by 42 percent, the number attending a political rally or speech by 34 percent, and the number writing to Congress by 23 percent. Likewise, 25 percent fewer Americans vote today than did so in the mid-sixties. Putnam fears that in politics, as in communities, Americans are becoming spectators rather than participants.

Daniel Kemmis, former mayor of Missoula, Montana, links democratic participation and social capital, although he refers to it as neighborliness: "It is in being good neighbors that people very often engage in those simple, homely practices which are the last, best hope for a revival of genuine public life. In valuing neighborliness, people value that upon which citizenship most essentially depends." As an example of neighborliness, Kemmis describes the barn-raising party that he observed as a young boy on his father's ranch. Unfortunately, barn raising these days is even less popular than are bowling leagues.

CRITIQUING BOWLING ALONE

The decline of barn raising and bowling leagues points to one of several problems with Putnam's analysis. He is tracking participation in many organizations and activities that are losing their relevance. Most of the organizations that Putnam tracks were founded a hundred or more years ago. The fact that people are leaving these organizations does not mean that these people are no longer engaged in their communities. My observations in Seattle over the past twenty-eight years lead me to conclude that people are finding new ways of connecting with one another.

There may be fewer people in bowling leagues today, but more people than ever are bowling together. My son, Joey, organized the Franklin Bowling Club at his high school. It brought together about seventy teenagers from all races and incomes. My guess is that it did more than any bowling league to create the kind of bridging (i.e., inclusive) social capital that Putnam advocates.

Similarly, Seattleites are finding replacements for other types of participation that Putnam describes as being on the wane. People may be spending less time in bars (and more time in meetings of a voluntary association known as Alcoholics Anonymous), but for every tavern that has closed, there are many—very many—more coffee shops that have opened. Seattleites may be participating in fewer dinner parties, but five thousand urban gardeners are growing food together in community gardens, and thousands more are meeting their neighbors and local producers by shopping at one of seven farmers' markets. Seattleites may not be raising barns, but tens of thousands have joined together to build parks, playgrounds, and other community amenities. Membership may be declining in the local NAACP chapter, but the Hate Free Zone, Northwest Immigrant Rights, and similar civil rights organizations have sprung up. Other new groups range from mutual assistance associations for recent immigrants, to block watches numbering four thousand, to dozens of neighborhood-based art, history, and environmental organizations. All of this has occurred within the past thirty-five years, when America's social capital was supposedly dwindling to its lowest point.

Seattleites may be spending less time in the voting booth and sending fewer letters to Congress, but that doesn't mean they have opted out of politics. Successful citizen initiatives restricted the height of downtown skyscrapers, preserved parks for public use, and secured funding for a monorail. Other grassroots campaigns led to a comprehensive recycling program, shut down nuclear power plants, and stopped a freeway from being built. Activists in the African American, Latino American, and Native American communities occupied and expropriated closed school buildings and a military base, which now serve as cultural centers. Seattleites took to the streets for massive demonstrations in support of gay rights and renaming a major boulevard for Martin Luther King Jr. and in protest of the World Trade Organization and various wars. They mobilized against the invasion of Iraq at the neighborhood level: hosting peace potlucks in their homes, sponsoring teach-ins at local community centers, waving signs in local business districts, staging candlelight vigils in local parks, and coming together in large citywide demonstrations, marching behind the banners of their neighborhoods. Instead of sending letters, they deluged their congressional representatives with e-mail messages. Such activities have definitely not been the staid politics of the 1950s, and a wealth of social capital has been generated.

That brings me to a second disagreement with Putnam's analysis. He seems more concerned with the quantity than the quality of participation. Putnam counts all participation the same and does little to distinguish the different roles or to weigh the relative value of the many forms that participation takes. As a result, he makes the strange assertion that "voluntary associations, from churches and professional associations to Elks Clubs and reading groups allow individuals to express their interests and demands on government and to protect themselves from abuses of power by the political leaders." Surely, though, the Elks Club and reading groups are not on a par with the Sierra Club and neighborhood associations when it comes to exercising political influence. And while Boy Scouts, gangs, militias, and the VFW are all voluntary associations, they do not play the same role in building community.

A third problem with Putnam's analysis is that it focuses more on individuals' actions than on the systems prompting individuals to take those actions. Putnam blames the breakdown of social capital on families working for a second income, moving to suburbs, and watching too much television, and on young adults in general. David Schultz characterizes Putnam as claiming that "the poor performance of a democracy is our fault—we do not participate, we do not engage, we do not do our duty in producing social capital." In *Social Capital: Critical Perspectives on Community and "Bowling Alone,"* Schultz and his colleagues instead attribute the erosion of democratic participation and social capital to the rapid expansion of corporate power, to globalization, and to unprecedented inequities in income.

Similarly, in their book on the Dudley Street Neighborhood Initiative (DSNI), *Streets of Hope,* Peter Medoff and Holly Sklar take issue with those who blame that Boston neighborhood's decline on its low-income residents. The residents weren't opting out of community participation, according to DSNI leader Paul Bothwell. Instead, the community "was torn limb from limb and heart from heart and person from person. . . . This is the result of city policy, of other kinds of large-scale things that systematically cripple or dismember a community." The authors identify those "large-scale things" as redlining by banks and insurance companies, blockbusting by realtors, arson by absentee landlords, urban renewal by government, and the failure of officials to crack down on illegal dumping and garbage transfer stations operating without permits. The problem wasn't that people were spending too much of their time at work, but rather that Stride Rite, a major employer in the neighborhood, had moved its factory to Asia. The issues were systemic and the community's future depended on a strategic, organized response—not random acts of neighborliness.

COMMUNITY ORGANIZING

"America is a vast laboratory of democratic experiments," writes Harry Boyte. "Even as we lament the loss of public life, it reappears in a myriad of forms, with intimations of a citizen politics for the future." Over the past third of a century, there have emerged three forms of participatory democracy that seem to me to be especially promising: asset-based community development, formal participation structures, and community organizing.

What we know today as community organizing originated with Saul Alinsky. Writing fifty years before *Bowling Alone*, Alinsky made observations similar to those of Robert Putnam about the breakdown of community life. "In our modern urban civilization," he wrote in *Reveille for Radicals*, "multitudes of our people have been condemned to urban anonymity—to living the kind of life where many of them neither know nor care about their own neighbors. . . . The course of urban anonymity, of individual divorce from the general social life, erodes the foundations of democracy."

Alinsky was determined to restore democracy for America's poor. While the "have-nots" lacked the power of money, Alinsky recognized that they had a potential strength that the rich lacked—the power of numbers. He believed that the best way to develop that power was for an outside agitator, the organizer, "to rub raw the sores of discontent." The organizer's job was to mobilize people around issues that were in their "self-interest" and that were "specific, immediate, and realizable." While understanding the importance of "operating within the experience of the people" being organized, Alinsky recognized the power of taking action that was outside the experience of the government official or corporate representative who was the "target." The goal was not simply to win victories to improve specific conditions, he wrote in *Rules for Radicals;* the goal was also "to build confidence and hope in the idea of organization." Alinsky sought to restore democracy and to effect social change by building ongoing "people's organizations."

Alinsky developed his approach to organizing in Chicago's impoverished Back of the Yards neighborhood, so-named because of its proximity to the stockyards. In 1938, he began organizing a broad-based coalition of fifty local organizations, including churches, small business, labor, and youth, to support meatpacking workers in their bid for union recognition. They succeeded. Alinsky then focused the attention of this coalition, called the Back of the Yards Neighborhood Council, on community issues. Borrowing strategies from organized labor, Alinsky used boycotts, sit-ins, and other confrontational tactics to help the residents win victories on issues ranging from health-care services to youth recreation programs.

Alinsky and his associates went on to organize other neighborhoods in Chicago and in communities as diverse as Butte, Montana; Rochester, New York; and the Mexican-American community of southern California. Although the organizations all achieved significant improvements for their communities, most of the organizations were short-lived. An exception was the Back of the Yards Neighborhood Council, but it became a great disappointment to Alinsky when its members opposed integration in the 1950s and endorsed George Wallace for president in 1968.

When Alinsky died in 1972, his work continued through the Industrial Areas Foundation (IAF), which he had established as a training institute. Ed Chambers, a veteran organizer and former seminarian, became the new director of the IAF. The IAF was attracting a young generation of civil rights and peace activists who had been inspired by Alinsky's writings and were eager to learn how to be effective organizers.

One of those young people was Ernesto Cortes. After being trained by the IAF in Chicago, Cortes returned to his hometown of San Antonio in 1973. He conducted more than a thousand one-on-one conversations with Roman Catholic priests and lay leaders that resulted in twenty-seven predominantly Hispanic parishes joining together to form Communities Organized for Public Service (COPS). The organization grew through ongoing relationship building, intensive discussions of values, and extensive training and mentoring combined with successful actions such as the disruption of business at a major San Antonio department store and at a bank. When COPS held its twenty-fifth annual convention in 1999, six thousand people turned out. They celebrated that COPS had secured well over $1 billion in improvements for their neighborhoods, including new schools, libraries, health clinics, roads, sewers, parks, affordable housing, and job training. By registering and mobilizing voters, COPS had also played major roles in defeating a tax limitation initiative, approving bond measures, passing a charter amendment for the election of city council members by district, and electing a Hispanic mayor.

Mark Warren, who wrote *Dry Bones Rattling* based on his field research on COPS between 1993 and 1999, attributes the extraordinary length, breadth, and depth of Cortes's success to several refinements he made to Alinsky's approach. First and foremost, Cortes took the relationship with the member churches seriously, integrating Christian values into the training and helping the churches themselves to become stronger organizations. Second, Cortes took to heart IAF's "Iron Rule" that an organizer must never do for the people what they can do for themselves; in COPS, it is the members themselves who identify the issues and do the recruiting, training, research, and strategizing. Third, although Cortes saw a more limited role for the organizer than Alinsky had seen, Cortes believed that there is an ongoing need for an organizer to ensure that the leadership doesn't become stale. Fourth, Cortes was not satisfied with empowering separate communities; he went on to build a multicultural, statewide organization with significant clout on major issues. Although Cortes still relies on Alinsky's fundamental principles, these innovations have contributed to a new model of community organizing.

Variations on the COPS model are taking root in most major and many smaller cities and even in rural areas throughout the United States. The IAF has sixty-two affiliate organizations stretching from Los Angeles to Brooklyn. The Pacific Institute for Community Organization originated in Oakland, California, in 1972 and has since become a congregation-based network of forty-four affiliates in fourteen states that reaches to Florida, Louisiana, and Alabama, where rural organizing is under way. Another network in the tradition of IAF is the Gamaliel Foundation, which has grown to include forty-five affiliates in seventeen states since it was founded in 1986. Thousands of congregations from many faiths and denominations are participating in these three networks.

There are about two dozen other national and regional organizing networks, most of which are secularly based. The largest of these is the Association of Community Organizations for Reform Now (ACORN). Founded in Arkansas in 1970, ACORN now has 150,000 individual members in seven hundred neighborhood chapters in fifty-one cities. Other prominent networks providing training and technical assistance include the Center for Third World Organizing and the National Training and Information Center.

FORMAL PARTICIPATION STRUCTURES

Mark Warren asserts that "revitalizing democracy requires effective connections between well-organized communities and our political system. As political parties have lost their base in communities, new forms of mediating institutions are needed that can hold public institutions . . . accountable to communities." Warren makes the case that COPS and similar coalitions of community organizations effectively play this intermediary role. What Warren fails to note is that many local governments are initiating their own connections to communities; this is a second form of participatory democracy that has emerged over the last three decades.

In *The Rebirth of Urban Democracy,* Jeffrey M. Berry, Kent E. Portney, and Ken Thomson analyze "strong democracy" programs in five cities that they researched from 1985 to 1992 as part of the National Citizen Participation Project at Tufts University. One of those programs was COPS in San Antonio, and the other four were programs sponsored by local government in Birmingham, Alabama; Dayton, Ohio; Portland, Oregon; and St. Paul, Minnesota. These municipal programs were initiated between 1971 and 1975 in response to federal Community Development Block Grant requirements and funding for citizen participation.

As described in the appendix to Ken Thomson's later *Neighborhoods to Nation,* each of the four government-sponsored programs divides the entire city into districts. District-level organizations serve as the intermediary linking city government to the neighborhoods. In Birmingham, voters within each of ninety-three neighborhoods go to the polls to elect three officers for their Neighborhood Association who, together with the officers of other Neighborhood Associations within their district ("Community"), constitute the membership of one of twenty-two Community Advisory Committees; the committees elect their own officers and representatives to a citywide Citizens Advisory Board. In Dayton, voters in each district ("Area") go to the polls to elect members of one of seven Priority Boards; these elected representatives, together with a much smaller number of representatives appointed by some of the neighborhood groups, elect a chair who sits on a citywide Chairpersons Council. In Portland, the Neighborhood Associations, together with a smaller number of other interests in each district, choose delegates for one of six District Coalition Boards; there is no citywide body representing all of the boards. In St. Paul, at annual meetings or at the polls, citizens within each district elect representatives who are in some cases joined by a smaller number of delegates chosen by neighborhood or business groups to sit on one of seventeen District Councils; there is no direct representation to a citywide body, although the mayor selects from the nominees of each District Council for membership on a Capital Improvement Budget Committee. St. Paul alone has no government-recognized neighborhood associations, so the District Councils are the first tier of St. Paul's citizen participation structure.

All four government-sponsored programs have enabled city government to be more responsive to the neighborhoods. Instead of city hall responding primarily to those neighborhoods that are the most affluent or the best organized, each of these cities has created a formal structure providing for access by all neighborhoods. Each program's structure decentralizes authority so that neighborhood representatives have a significant voice in local land-use issues and in some level of city budget allocations; St. Paul's budget process is the most advanced, with the elected District Councils nominating all members of the committee that develops and recommends the city's entire capital improvement budget. All four cities have regular channels for two-way communication between the neighborhoods and city hall. Each of the citywide bodies facilitates a healthy exchange of ideas, information, and perspectives across neighborhoods. The official neighborhood representatives in all of the cities receive government resources for organizational staff support and outreach to their constituencies.

Although these cities' programs have proven track records, several observers have raised questions about this form of participatory democracy. In some ways, it seems less participatory and more an extension of representative democracy. Most of the district representatives in St. Paul and Dayton are elected at the polls or in annual meetings, so they have no direct ties to neighborhood associations or other community organizations. In fact, Berry and his colleagues found that Dayton's "second tier Priority Boards tend to dominate or in some ways compete with the neighborhood level of representation." Also, the Tufts researchers concluded that the number of active citizens in these cities is no greater than in cities with similar demographics but lacking such programs. Other observers, as cited by Frances Moore Lappé and Paul Martin DuBois, have questioned whether grassroots activists can retain sufficient independence when city government not only establishes neighborhood boundaries but certifies neighborhood associations and furnishes much of their staff support and funding.

Despite these questions and criticisms, it is clear to all observers that this new form of democracy is a positive development in terms of bringing decision-making closer to the people. Moreover, it's catching on. About 40 percent of cities with a population of more than a hundred thousand had officially recognized neighborhood associations in 1990, according to *Civic Innovation in America* (Sirianni and Friedland, 2001), and that percentage appears to be increasing. *Government Is Us* (King and Stivers, 1998) and *The Quickening of America* (Lappé and DuBois, 1994) describe the success of other jurisdictions—from small towns in Orange County, Florida, to cities like Chattanooga, Phoenix, and Roanoke—in generating broad-based participation through community visioning and similar planning processes.

ASSET-BASED COMMUNITY DEVELOPMENT

A third form of participatory democracy requires no government involvement at all. In fact, its chief proponent, John McKnight, argues that asset-based community development typically has been inhibited by government. Government, like social service agencies and other institutions, tends to disempower communities by focusing on their deficiencies and fostering dependence on outside interventions. Asset-based community development, on the other hand, builds on the resources that are found in every community. These assets include a community's associations and all its members, even those members who have been labeled and dismissed: the disabled, welfare mothers, at-risk youth, and elderly; all persons of every description have skills, knowledge, and passion to contribute to their community. McKnight would never refer to anyone as a "have-not."

McKnight, who organized Chicago neighborhoods in the early 1960s, is another who received his training from Saul Alinsky. Alinsky railed against what he called "welfare colonialism." "Self-respect arises only out of people who play an active role in solving their own crises and who are not helpless, passive, puppet-like recipients of private or public services," he wrote in *Rules for Radicals*. "To give people help, while denying them a significant part in the action, contributes nothing to the development of the individual. In the deepest sense it is not giving but taking—taking their dignity."

McKnight shared Alinsky's perspective on the dangers of doing for people what they can do for themselves, but he came to believe that Alinsky did not go far enough in implementing the so-called Iron Rule of organizing. Empowering communities to demand more services from government was not sufficient. Truly empowered communities, claims McKnight in *The Careless Society,* are those that identify, connect, and utilize their own assets.

Asset-based community development contributes not solely to the dignity of the individual but also to the vitality of a neighborhood and ultimately to the health of democracy. For individuals, it offers genuine care, not impersonal services. For neighborhoods, it creates a strong sense of community; takes a holistic, community-directed approach to development; and builds on sustainable and formerly underutilized resources. As for democracy, asset-based community development transforms passive clients and customers into active citizens, creating what Lappé and DuBois call a "living democracy"—one that is present in all arenas of people's lives and not bound by institutions.

McKnight collaborated with John "Jody" Kretzmann on *Building Communities from the Inside Out,* a book filled with inspiring examples of how asset-based community development can contribute to a living democracy. One of their examples is the Dudley Street Neighborhood Initiative, further documented by Medoff and Sklar as mentioned earlier. *Streets of Hope* identifies the external forces responsible for Boston's most distressed neighborhood. More crucially, it demonstrates "that low-income communities have extensive resources—from multilingual residents, local businesspeople and family day care providers to underemployed people, underutilized land and school facilities, and children with dreams and talents to share."

The Dudley Street Neighborhood Initiative utilized these local resources for a community-driven revitalization campaign that began in 1986. Working through existing community organizations, DSNI focused on transforming the neighborhood's more than 1,300 vacant lots from a problem into an asset. The community conducted neighborhood cleanups while successfully pressuring city government to enforce its ordinances on illegal dumping and abandoned cars. While still in its first year of operation, DSNI initiated a participatory, comprehensive planning process for human, economic, and physical development. The land-use component called for developing the vacant lots as an urban village complete with housing, community centers, parks, businesses, and a town commons. Thanks to widespread participation in the planning process and broad-based community support for the vision that resulted, Mayor Ray Flynn was persuaded not only to adopt the plan but to confer on DSNI the unprecedented power of eminent domain. DSNI proceeded to establish a community land trust and to work with its local partners to build permanently affordable housing. A group of youth, ages eight to nineteen, took the lead in designing their new community center, and the community as a whole participated in charettes for the town commons. Meanwhile, DSNI organized a nine-week-long Community Summerfest complete with youth recreation programs and a community-wide multicultural festival as a means to liberate a key park from control by drug dealers. DSNI also launched People and Resources Investing in Dudley's Environment (PRIDE), a block-by-block organizing effort to involve residents in supporting one another, maintaining their neighborhood, planting street trees, creating community gardens, enhancing public safety, and otherwise promoting Dudley PRIDE.

BRINGING IT ALL TOGETHER

I feel fortunate to have had extensive experience with all three forms of participatory democracy described here. From 1976 to 1982, I worked as a community organizer trained by Tom Gaudette, a close associate of Saul Alinsky's, and under the direction of Greg Galluzzo, currently director of the Gamaliel Foundation. Between 1982 and 1988, the nation's largest health-care cooperative employed me to help establish and staff a system of consumer-elected medical center councils and regional councils with responsibilities for budget development and quality of care oversight similar to the formal participation structures of Birmingham, Dayton, Portland, and St. Paul. That experience led me to Seattle city government, where I served as the first director of the Department of Neighborhoods from 1988 until 2002. During that time, I was invited to describe Seattle's programs in many other cities and at conferences where I frequently crossed paths with John McKnight and Jody Kretzmann; in 2002, they invited me to join the faculty of their Asset-Based Community Development Institute.

Mindful of the strengths and limitations of the three forms of participatory democracy discussed here, I tried to integrate the best features of each as Seattle's Department of Neighborhoods was first created and over the years expanded and evolved. The need for an asset-based approach was clear to me, especially in light of the fact that increasingly complex social issues were quickly outstripping Seattle city government's capacity to respond. Rather than being a barrier to such an approach, it seemed to me, government could play a useful catalytic role. No less clear to me was the importance of preserving the independence of neighborhood associations and of building the capacity of organizations representing historically disenfranchised populations, so that they could demand fair treatment by government and other outside forces affecting their communities.

Following is the story of the first fourteen years of Seattle's Department of Neighborhoods. That story testifies to the remarkable achievements that communities can accomplish when government takes its democratic foundations as seriously as it does its responsibilities for streets, public safety, and other services. Through the Department of

Neighborhoods, tens of thousands of people have become active in their communities and with their government, often for the first time. Working together, citizens have been planning, building community projects, gardening, developing new and more capable organizations, bridging neighborhoods and cultures, and influencing city hall. If Putnam's statistics are right, fewer people have been practicing democracy's historic forms, but, in Seattle and across the nation, more people are engaged in the newer forms of participatory democracy that have evolved to meet the needs of our present society.

1
VALUING COMMUNITY
The Department of Neighborhoods' Origins

ocal governments throughout the United States are facing a dual dilemma. Their resources are not keeping pace with increasingly complex social issues, especially when the federal and state governments are devolving more responsibilities than money to them. Voters are reluctant to approve additional resources because they feel a sense of alienation from their government at all levels.

The common response has been to "reinvent government" to be more like a business with a greater emphasis on efficiency and customer service. Although it is true that government needs to improve its business practices, there is a danger inherent in treating citizens as customers. To the extent that government treats citizens only as customers, citizens think of themselves only as taxpayers and feel that much more alienated from their government.

This deep sense of alienation is often misdiagnosed as apathy. Statistics showing that fewer and fewer people are voting and are joining community organizations have led some to the conclusion that increasing numbers of citizens no longer care about their community or their government. This analysis, I believe, blames the victim. Citizens don't vote because they have seen little evidence that their votes matter. The 2000 presidential election only confirmed what so many people already suspected: their votes didn't count. Likewise, people hesitate to join community organizations because they are tired of attending meetings that lead to nothing but more meetings. Whether they are participating in a planning workshop or a discussion of bylaws, too many people have a hard time seeing a positive relationship between their civic involvement and the quality of their lives.

I am convinced that people still yearn for a sense of community and want to contribute to the greater good. They also want a voice in their government. What they are looking for has less to do with reinventing government than it does with rediscovering democracy. True democracy requires deeper involvement than going to the voting booth once a year; people need to be engaged in their communities and with their government on an ongoing basis. People will commit to such involvement to the extent that they see results.

I say this with confidence because of the high level of citizen engagement I witnessed in Seattle between 1988 and 2002. Tens of thousands of people participated in implementing more than two thousand community self-help projects such as building new parks and playgrounds, renovating community facilities, recording oral histories, and creating public art. Thirty thousand people guided the development of thirty-seven neighborhood plans. Scores of new ethnic organizations and neighborhood-based residential, business, arts, history, and environmental organizations were established. Five thousand people a year were involved in cultivating plots at sixty-two community gardens that they built themselves. Organizations celebrated an annual Neighbor Appreciation Day, and individuals delivered eighteen thousand greeting cards to caring neighbors. Many people with developmental disabilities and other formerly marginalized citizens participated in community life for the first time. These are some of the many activities that accounted for survey results showing that 43 percent of Seattle's adults regularly volunteered their time for the community and 62 percent participated in at least one neighborhood or community organization.

Civic engagement created additional resources for the public good. P-Patch community garden volunteers generated ten tons of organic produce for food banks each year and maintained more than seventeen acres of public space. Community members invested more than $30 million worth of their own cash, materials, and labor in completing more than two thousand projects that they initiated. Likewise, broad-based ownership of the thirty-seven neighborhood plans led to voter approval of three ballot measures worth $470 million for library, community center, and park improvements recommended in the plans.

Perhaps more important than the financial and other material benefits of civic engagement are the social benefits of a stronger sense of community. No amount of public-safety spending can buy the kind of security that comes from neighbors watching out for one another. Similarly, neighbors supporting latchkey children or housebound seniors can provide a kind of personal care that social service agencies can't replicate.

There are other things that communities can do better than government can. Community members have local knowledge and can provide a local perspective. At the same time, they think more holistically than government departments that tend to specialize in specific functions.

The community is often more innovative than the city bureaucracy and can constitute a powerful force for change. When the City of Seattle planned to build incinerators to deal with its garbage problem, the community demanded a recycling program instead. When electricity rates escalated after the city bought into a nuclear power project, the community pushed for a model conservation program. It was the community that introduced the Seattle Police Department to community policing and insisted on its implementation.

Likewise, the community has power where city government does not. The city couldn't persuade the Seattle School District to host community school programs, but the community did. Government couldn't evict a pornographer from the sole theater in Seattle's Columbia City neighborhood, but the community did.

None of this is meant to suggest that there is no role for government. While the community provides a local perspective, government must look citywide to ensure that neighborhoods are connected and that each is treated equitably. Community innovation needs to be balanced by a certain amount of government standards and regulations. My point is simply that cities work best when local government and the community are working as partners.

True partnership requires government to move beyond promoting citizen participation to facilitating community empowerment. Citizen participation implies government involving citizens in its own priorities through its own processes (such as public hearings and task forces) and programs (such as block watch and adopt-a-street). Community empowerment, on the other hand, means giving citizens the tools and resources they need to address their own priorities through their own organizations.

In 1988, the City of Seattle had long been known, if seldom commended, for its emphasis on process. That year, the city made a sea change toward community empowerment with the creation of a four-person Office of Neighborhoods. The office quickly grew into a department that, by 2002, had nearly a hundred employees and a budget of $12 million a year. The Department of Neighborhoods differs from other city departments that are responsible for separate functions such as transportation, public safety, human services, or parks and recreation. Neighborhoods is the only department focused on the way citizens have organized themselves: by community. That unique focus enables the department to decentralize and coordinate city services, to cultivate a greater sense of community and nurture broad-based community organizations, and to work in partnership with these organizations to improve neighborhoods by building on each one's special character.

In subsequent chapters, I describe the department's programs to empower communities and recount stories that show some of the ways that citizens have used those programs to strengthen their organizations and neighborhoods. First, however, I want to describe how Seattle's elected officials came to create an Office of Neighborhoods and how I came to be its first director.

MY JOURNEY TO THE CITY OF SEATTLE

I arrived at my position with the City of Seattle via a rusty orange 1971 Volkswagen squareback. After graduating from college in the small town of Grinnell, Iowa, my wife, Sarah Driggs, and I looked at a map of the United States to help us decide where to make our first home. We were captivated by the concentration of blue and green in the northwest corner of the map and decided to move to Seattle. We bought the VW, loaded our few possessions into the back, and headed west. Having had little experience with a stick shift, we finally wrestled it into fourth gear and kept to the freeway as much as possible.

The map hadn't prepared us for the fact that Seattle is built on seven hills. We needed a home and found ourselves looking for an apartment on the steep slopes of Queen Anne and Capitol Hill. We needed money, and our job hunt took us through the heavy traffic of downtown, where we struggled to parallel park on equally steep slopes. Feeling hassled, lost, and anonymous in this city of half a million, we almost decided to keep moving to a smaller town.

Then we found an apartment in Wallingford, a neighborhood near the center of the city, just north of Lake Union. Our neighbors greeted us and made us feel at home. We soon became acquainted with the merchants in Wallingford's business district. We attended meetings of the Wallingford Community Council and discovered that we weren't so powerless after all. Wallingford, with a population of about six thousand, had a scale and feel not unlike Grinnell's.

It was in Wallingford that I discovered what it is that makes Seattle such a great place to live. Outsiders know Seattle for the Space Needle, Pike Place Market, and SAFECO Field; for Mount Rainier and Puget Sound; for Boeing, Microsoft, and REI; for the General Strike of 1919 and the anti-WTO demonstrations of 1999; for Jimi Hendrix and Kurt Cobain; for salmon and coffee; and for the incessant rain. But it's certainly not the rain that keeps most people in Seattle. I came to see that Seattle's greatest asset is the strong sense of community that comes from our vibrant neighborhoods. When you ask Seattleites where they live, they frequently answer with the name of their neighborhood: Alki, Ballard, Capitol Hill, Delridge, Eastlake, Fremont, Greenwood, Haller Lake, the International District, and so on.

Seattle has about a hundred neighborhoods. They are typically defined by the city's topography of hills, valleys, and bodies of water. Each neighborhood usually has a business district and a public elementary school. The average neighborhood—although there is really no such thing as an average neighborhood in Seattle—has about five thousand residents.

Virtually every neighborhood is represented by some form of a community council and often has a business association as well. These grass-roots organizations, which advocate on issues, organize events, and sponsor projects, are independent of city government and independent of one another. The 1928 *Handbook and Directory of the Federated Northeast Clubs of Seattle* lists many of the same organizations that exist today.

When Sarah and I moved to Seattle in 1976, though, there were still some neighborhoods that lacked community councils. The neighborhoods with the greatest needs seemed to be the least organized to effect change. Given my long-standing interest in working for social justice and my newfound appreciation for community, I decided that my first job (aside from cleaning the Kingdome's restrooms on its opening day) would be as a community organizer.

I went to work for a Saul Alinsky–style organizing project started by two Jesuit priests in the low-income, racially diverse neighborhoods of Rainier Valley, Beacon Hill, and Georgetown. My fellow organizers and I canvassed door-to-door looking for potential issues and leaders that could serve as the basis for creating local neighborhood organizations.

Typically, I would introduce myself and ask if there were any problems in the neighborhood. All too often the response would be, "You can't fight city hall" or "Why, are you a lawyer?" In other words, politicians and lawyers were the only ones with power. We tried to give people a sense that they could create their own power by banding together around a common cause. It was a difficult job because people felt isolated and powerless.

One of our first organizing efforts was in the Empire-Kenyon Apartments. In our canvassing, we heard complaints about rent and utility rate increases, substandard housing conditions, rats, the lack of play equipment, and the need for a crosswalk signal on the adjacent street, a busy thoroughfare. The tenants felt so overwhelmed by all of these problems that it was difficult to bring them together around any one issue.

Then one day a child was killed while using the striped crosswalk on the busy street. We organized a community meeting and invited the Engineering Department. "What will it take before we can get a signal installed?" the chair demanded of the city representative. "Another death?" "No, two deaths" was the response. "We have standards."

The community was so incensed that, the next day, people formed a steady stream of pedestrians, walking back and forth in the crosswalk, backing up traffic for blocks. The fliers they handed to the waiting motorists read: "Sorry for the inconvenience. We need a light to get traffic moving again." The flier asked people to call the head of the Engineering Department—and gave his home phone number—to request a light. Shortly thereafter a traffic light was installed.

Similar tactics were employed in other neighborhoods. When Dunlap neighbors couldn't get the Building Department to inspect an illegal dump being created by a contractor, they removed a gigantic boulder from the accumulating pile and hauled it to city hall, where they dumped it in the director's office. When elderly and disabled tenants from Holly Park couldn't get Metro Transit to build a shelter at their bus stop, they invited newspaper and television reporters to come watch them build one for themselves. Angry tenants in the Gale Place Apartments converged on and surrounded the waterfront home of a slum landlord, some arriving by bus and the rest by boat. Six hundred neighbors and union members marched across the rickety South Lucile Street Bridge to a meeting with elected officials, where they demanded that the failing structure be replaced. A Seattle School Board meeting was interrupted by Chinese American students from Cleveland High School performing what they feared would be their last lion dance, because students of color were being bused to other schools. When the mayor, under pressure from the federal department of Housing and Urban Development, backed down on a campaign commitment, a community delegation released a chicken in his office.

Although these and other actions were successful in effecting change, the victories were not the ultimate goal. The goal was to use the victories to build ongoing neighborhood groups so that the power that had been developed through each issue campaign could be sustained and applied to other issues. Once several neighborhood groups had been established, we brought them together with local churches to form the South End Seattle Community Organization. SESCO grew to include twenty-six member groups over the six years that I worked for it as an organizer and director. As many as eight hundred people attended annual

Hundreds march to demand the construction of a new Lucile Street Bridge. Photograph by Ron DeRosa, Seattle Times; reprinted with permission.

conventions at which the members elected officers and voted on community-wide issues that they wanted to work on together. Among those projects was a fight against garbage incinerators, which led to a city-wide recycling program, opposition to the overconcentration of low-income housing, which resulted in a scattered-site housing program, and a local ratepayers' revolt by SESCO's Light Brigade, which quickly grew into a successful statewide campaign against nuclear power.

My experience with SESCO taught me three valuable lessons about organizing that have guided my work ever since. The first is to start where people are. Most important, this means organizing people around what interests them rather than around what you think they should be interested in. It also means respecting people's culture and communicating in their language, utilizing existing networks instead of trying to create your own, and meeting with people where they are accustomed to gathering.

The second lesson is to organize people around issues that are immediate, concrete, and achievable. It's difficult to bring together community people to do long-range planning, to address a vague problem like "public safety," or to take on a huge issue like nuclear disarmament, but it is relatively easy to bring together people for a specific, achievable task to address an immediate issue, for instance, to plan a course of action to remove violent video games from a local arcade following a neighborhood shooting. Once people have a sense of power because they have succeeded with small issues, they are readier to tackle issues that are larger and take longer.

The third lesson is one that my mentor, Tom Gaudette, drilled into me: "Organizers organize organizations." The organizer's role is to build an organization, not to be the leader in winning an issue. Issues are one tool that the organizer can use to develop leadership and help build the organization so that it is broad based and self-sufficient. The best organizers don't foster dependency; they work their way out of their jobs.

I took these lessons with me to Group Health Cooperative in 1982. Group Health had been founded in 1947 by members who mortgaged their homes and by physicians who were ostracized by the medical establishment because they wanted to create a cooperative to make health care affordable to the working class. By 1982 Group Health had grown to become the nation's largest health care cooperative, with more than 300,000 consumers, and had begun to lose sight of the very thing that set it apart: membership ownership and participation. To try to reengage members in the governance of their organization, the cooperative's board of trustees created a Cooperative Affairs Department. As an employee of Cooperative Affairs, I worked to build membership-based groups: medical center councils that reviewed clinic budgets and quality of care, special interest groups for seniors and antinuclear activists, and Partners for Health, a group supporting a sister clinic in Managua, Nicaragua. I also staffed the annual membership meetings, which attracted as many as 2,500 people. I was intent on making the cooperative more responsive to its members, becoming a model for the nationalized health care I hoped was on the horizon.

Our department was able to do this work as part of management, because we took extreme care not to cross the line between organizer and leader. We never advocated the positions of management or of the membership. Instead, we made it possible for managers, medical providers, and members to work together.

In 1988, I got the opportunity to develop a similar model for the City of Seattle. Mayor Charles Royer appointed me the first director of the new Office of Neighborhoods. This was the same mayor whose house I had picketed and whose office we had be-fowled during my time at SESCO. I never did figure out why he hired me, but clearly, he was no chicken after all.

My first days on the job rid me of a couple of other misconceptions. I quickly learned that my stereotype of bureaucrats as uncaring and lazy was largely untrue. People tend to work for city government because they want to be of service to the community, and the bureaucrats I met worked very hard. I did see that many good public servants are trapped in bad systems, and saw too that they are as frustrated as the people they are trying to serve.

I learned another important lesson by attending the mayor's annual cabinet retreat my first week on the job. I had always wondered how the power structure worked: Whose decision was it to treat the community of Southeast Seattle as second class? I thought that the cabinet retreat would be a good opportunity to learn the secret.

With the Office of Neighborhoods just established, the retreat focused on how the city could do a better job of responding to neighborhood issues. We discussed the growing drug and gang problem and concluded that the city had already tried nearly every solution that money could buy. Affordable housing was a major neighborhood issue, but there was little the city could do, especially when the state legislature had outlawed rent control. Likewise, the city had no jurisdiction over the schools, whose decline was having a major impact on the neighborhoods. Traffic congestion and inadequate parking were equally perplexing.

I quickly realized that public officials felt as powerless to address these issues as did the citizens. Perhaps city government could come up with some new solutions as well as the power to implement them by working in partnership with neighborhood organizations—at least that was the thinking of some elected officials and community activists who had advocated the creation of the Office of Neighborhoods.

In a less collaborative era, Fremont merchants erected this rocket and aimed it at city hall. Photograph by Bradley Enghaus, Pacific Publishing; reprinted with permission.

HOW NEIGHBORHOODS BECAME A DEPARTMENT

There was little cooperation between neighborhood organizations and city government in the 1980s. Neighborhood organizations tended to be reactive and focused on single issues. SESCO was definitely the feistiest of the organizations, but community councils throughout Seattle were not shy about taking issue with city government on everything from crime to zoning. Increasingly in the 1980s, and especially in near–North End neighborhoods such as Ballard and Fremont, the issue was growth. Cherished open spaces and single-family neighborhoods were giving way to out-of-scale and badly designed apartment buildings that exacerbated Seattle's traffic and parking problems. Old neighborhood groups were getting reenergized, and new ones were forming. They opposed the city's plans to rezone for increased density and developers' proposals to build projects not in keeping with the character of their neighborhoods. Typically, the struggle took the groups from community meetings to the hearing examiner, to Seattle City Council hearings, and on to the courts. Neighborhood groups, developers, and city officials all were spending more time and money than they could afford in adversarial processes and were getting results that satisfied no one. Finally, city councilmember Jim Street, who chaired the Land Use Committee, got together with neighborhood activists and came up with a better solution: neighborhood planning. Rather than argue about particular development projects after they had been designed, why not involve the community from the start in planning for how best to accommodate growth?

In October 1986, the Seattle City Council allocated $40,000 to the city's Planning Commission to design a neighborhood planning program for Seattle. The commission hired consultants who assessed the city's existing organization and programs as well as those of other cities. The district council systems of Portland, Oregon, and St. Paul, Minnesota, especially interested the consultants.

Meanwhile, by holding public hearings and conducting surveys, the Planning Commission learned that neighborhood leaders had concerns other than too much growth. In fact, some economically distressed neighborhoods were desperate for growth. Gangs and drugs were mounting concerns in many communities. Citizen activists in every neighborhood shared a common concern that city hall wasn't working with them. They charged that too many resources were going to large downtown projects and not enough to the neighborhoods.

The Planning Commission broadened the scope of the study accordingly and in July 1987 submitted to the mayor and city council its "Recommendations on Neighborhood Planning and Assistance." That paper proposed to make Neighborhood Service Centers available throughout Seattle, create a system of district councils, expand resources for neighborhood planning, establish a neighborhood self-help fund (which came to be called the Neighborhood Matching Fund), increase neighborhood participation in the city's budget process, form an interdepartmental coordinating committee, and provide for improved notification to neighborhoods. Despite some objections from Mayor Royer and four of the nine councilmembers, Street was able to win approval for a resolution in October 1987 "to create a partnership between the City and its neighborhoods in order to provide the neighborhoods with tools and resources for planning and development which reflect their needs and values." The resolution established a Neighborhood Planning and

Assistance Program based largely on the Planning Commission recommendations. The resolution also created the Office of Neighborhoods to implement the program.

I hired an administrative assistant and two program managers, and the four-person Office of Neighborhoods began operating in April 1988. Three staff members were added in 1989, largely to help organize the neighborhoods that lacked strong community councils. When Norm Rice became mayor in 1990, he created the Department of Neighborhoods by consolidating the Office of Neighborhoods, Neighborhood Service Centers, and the Citizens Service Bureau. The Department of Neighborhoods was joined by the preexisting Office of Urban Conservation in 1992, the P-Patch Program in 1997, and the Neighborhood Planning Office in 1998. As the department grew, it shaped and integrated these programs to support a mission of "preserving and enhancing Seattle's diverse neighborhoods, empowering people to make positive contributions in their communities, and bringing government closer to all people, ensuring that it is responsive."

Community is at the core of the Department of Neighborhoods' mission, and it is the focus of every chapter in this book. Each chapter describes how one or more of the department's programs support a particular activity that contributes to strong, vibrant communities. A logical place to start is with community organizing, so that is the subject of the next chapter.

2

ORGANIZING COMMUNITIES
Involving All Neighbors and Other Programs

The Neighborhood Leadership Program of the Department of Neighborhoods offers classes and consultative services to help neighborhood activists develop effective organizations. That idea seemed sufficiently innovative to warrant a profile in *The Christian Science Monitor* (April 3, 1997) and sufficiently paradoxical to run under the headline "Mayors Train Activists How to Beat Up on City Hall."

Like the writers at *The Monitor,* elected officials in many cities are perplexed that Seattle city government encourages neighborhood activism. They see neighborhood activists as more of a problem than an asset. And that is understandable if they're thinking of the same handful of activists, self-proclaimed neighborhood leaders, whose mouths are bigger than their constituencies. Every city seems to have them, and Seattle is no exception. These activists are hard to please, and their pleasure with elected officials is usually short-lived. They are Lone Rangers who have little influence with the electorate, however, and most politicians have learned to discount them. But these activists tend not to be easily discouraged.

Unfortunately, elected officials often respond to the persistence of self-appointed leaders by becoming less democratic themselves. They can develop a bunker mentality and try to insulate themselves from the public. They can and often do try to wear down the activists with meaningless public process. Such a charade of public participation is costly in terms of time and money and even costlier in terms of community relations. Worse, it fails to take advantage of the abundant and power-ful assets that the community has to offer.

The solution, I believe, is to strive for more participation, not less. The best antidote to self-proclaimed neighborhood leaders is the pres-ence of broad-based community organizations. Democratic organiza-tions hold their leaders accountable, and they discredit those who falsely claim to speak for their community. Broad-based organizations are worth listening to because they are the electorate. They make it easy for elected officials to stay in touch with their constituents. The more representative the organization, the more beneficial it can be to city government.

Community organizations can contribute immeasurably more to city government than a link to the electorate, however. They can mobilize the valuable resources that are in every neighborhood: time, money, materials, skills, knowledge, pride, relationships. There is a great deal that communities can do that government cannot do, and there is even more that communities and government can accomplish by working together as true partners.

That is why it is in government's interest to help communities build their own organizations. In doing so, government must provide the tools and resources to enable all communities to have strong, representative organizations. Some communities will need more help than others. Too often, the communities with the greatest needs are the communities that are the least organized.

At the same time, government must be especially careful to help com-munity organizations in ways that do not jeopardize the organizations' independence. Communities will not be empowered if their organiza-tions are beholden to government or are in other ways dependent on external resources. Only truly empowered communities can engage in true partnerships with government.

This book describes several programs in the Department of Neigh-borhoods that help build self-sufficient, broad-based community organ-izations. Most of the department's programs have other goals as well, so this chapter focuses on those programs whose primary purpose is to help communities get organized.

BUILDING COMMUNITY ORGANIZATIONS

Seattle certainly had its share of community organizations before the Department of Neighborhoods arrived on the scene. In fact, there were already thousands of organizations: community councils, merchants associations, ethnic organizations, and special purpose groups such as block watches, parent/teacher associations, and service clubs. Low-income neighborhoods often lacked community councils, however, and most neighborhood-based groups tended to be whiter and wealthier than the communities they claimed to represent.

I wanted to ensure that all neighborhoods had access to Department of Neighborhoods programs, so I recruited a former Black Panther activist and the former director of Washington Fair Share to work as community organizers. Garry Owens and Dave Bockmann concentrated their efforts in the Central Area and Rainier Valley, where, at the invitation of local activists, they helped build community councils in eight low-income, multiethnic neighborhoods that previously had none. They were assisted in some of these neighborhoods by the drug dealers and gang members who, without intending to, had mobilized residents to take back their neighborhoods. Owens and Bockmann worked with emerging neighborhood leaders to tap into citizen anger and channel it to develop effective, ongoing community councils.

At the same time, we recognized that it wasn't sufficient to organize a community council for every neighborhood. Many communities, and immigrant/refugee communities in particular, are based more on a common culture than they are on common geography. So we also worked with East African and Southeast Asian communities to help organize mutual assistance associations. One such organization, Helping Link, was established by Vietnamese students from the University of Washington in 1993 and continues to offer classes in English, citizenship, and computers; mentoring and tutoring programs for youth; and cultural celebrations, including the Tet in Seattle festival. The organization has only one staff person, but it logs more than five thousand volunteer hours each year.

We went on to help existing community organizations throughout

Seattle develop broader memberships. Our work was grounded in the basic principles of community organizing. We started where the people were, in terms of their networks and in terms of their self-interest. We helped the community focus on goals that were immediate, concrete, and achievable. Always, we were very clear that our role was to provide advice and build leadership, not to be the leaders ourselves.

In 1990, the new chair of the Lake City Community Council asked me to advise her group on outreach strategies. I arrived at their meeting a little early, to find three members already in attendance. Fifteen minutes later, when no one else had joined us, I asked how many more people they were expecting. "None," one long-time member said with disgust. "We've been trying for years to get a new community center, but no one will help us. This community is so apathetic."

"Why do you think Lake City needs a new community center?" I asked.

"It seems obvious," the veteran member replied. "If we had a larger meeting room, we could attract more members."

I didn't question that logic, but I did ask if they had solicited the help of other neighborhood organizations in Lake City. "There aren't any others," another member said. "We're the only community council."

"Are there any churches in Lake City?" I asked. "Any schools, business organizations, tenants associations, service clubs, hobby clubs, crime prevention groups, senior centers, youth groups, sports teams? And what about the Vigilantes, the group that sponsors Lake City's annual Pioneer Days?" We had soon compiled a list of nearly fifty organizations in the neighborhood.

I suggested that we learn what these organizations cared about by inviting them to a town meeting. We divided up the list and each member took responsibility for personally inviting her third of the organizations. We thought that it would boost attendance to have a prominent speaker, so the council chair invited the mayor.

About 150 people turned out for the town meeting six weeks later. Mayor Rice, the former president of the Mount Baker Community Club, spoke about the importance of neighborhood activism and the many ways in which the city was prepared to partner with the community. Everyone then divided into small groups to identify Lake City's most pressing needs, and participants signed up to work on the issues that most interested them.

Over the next several years, hundreds of people were involved in successfully lobbying for a family support center, a late-night recreation program, and restrictions on billboards; organizing block watches; and building a school playground and a new park. The membership of the community council has ebbed and flowed since then, but the networking that began with that town meeting in 1990 has continued. Community members have worked together to develop a neighborhood plan, food bank, farmers' market, and large new park; to get new sidewalks; and to secure funding for a civic center complete with a new Neighborhood Service Center and an expanded library and community center.

INVOLVING ALL NEIGHBORS

In addition to advising individual community organizations, the Department of Neighborhoods offers citywide training workshops for grassroots leaders. Workshop topics include how to form an organization, facilitate meetings, set goals, win issue campaigns, work with the city, mediate disputes, manage projects, and raise funds. The crucial matter of outreach is addressed by sessions on membership recruitment, newsletter production, media strategies, and building inclusive organizations.

At one of our workshops in 1994, a panel of guest speakers discussed outreach to underrepresented populations, including newly arrived immigrants, youth, and tenants. As facilitator, I was helping field questions from participants. One participant, a woman named Carolyn Carlson, said she had a question for me. "What about outreach to people with developmental disabilities?"

I opened my mouth to answer and realized I had nothing to say. "I don't know," I said. "Maybe we can make that group the focus of a future workshop." I wasn't even sure what exactly developmental disabilities were.

Carlson approached me after the workshop and we scheduled a time to talk. When we met for coffee, she started telling me about her work supporting people with developmental disabilities. I interrupted and asked her to define developmental disabilities. Carlson gave me the stan-

dard working definition of "any mental and/or physical disability starting before age twenty-two and continuing indefinitely." She described
how, in past decades, people labeled as being developmentally disabled
had been placed in large institutions and how, in recent times, increasing numbers of these persons reside in group homes, with their families, or in their own apartments. Although thousands of persons with
developmental disabilities were living in Seattle neighborhoods in the
1990s, Carlson told me, very few were engaged in community life. As
a group within the community and as individuals, Carlson explained,
persons with developmental disabilities all too often ended up being
invisible. And, she added, the isolation and exclusion they experience
can be devastating.

Carlson believed that not only the person but the entire neighborhood gets shortchanged when someone with developmental disabilities
is not involved in his or her community. From her own experience, she
knew that persons with disabilities also have wonderful abilities: skills,
knowledge, creativity, and personalities that could enrich any neighborhood that welcomed them. A welcoming neighborhood, in turn, could
contribute greatly to the quality of life for those individuals. We decided
to initiate a pilot project to explore how best to involve persons with
developmental disabilities in a neighborhood organization.

Our efforts focused on Fremont, where the neighborhood council had
recently established Fremont Time, a volunteer-run service exchange
network to provide a structure for community inclusion. The organization catalogued the skills of participating members, helped members
utilize one another's services, and tracked the number of hours each
member contributed. All skills were valued equally, so every hour a member contributed made that person eligible to receive an hour of another
member's services.

We assisted Fremont Time in recruiting individuals with developmental disabilities. Once their skills and interests had been identified,
the new Fremont Time member was generally matched with another
member with similar interests to form an exchange team. Team members provided their services together. For example, one team provided
gardening services so that the team member with disabilities could obtain
art lessons from another member; in time, a relationship developed and

Lupita Cano tells her story as Joe Adcock listens and records. Photograph by Carolyn Carlson.

the two began spending time together "off the books," creating greeting cards. Other exchange teams moved furniture, painted houses, and helped with office work in an elementary school.

One notable exchange involved Joe Adcock, a professional journalist, and Lupita Cano, an extremely creative woman with Down syndrome. They met weekly to write Cano's journal, a narrative that grew to include hundreds of entries. In exchange for his transcription services, Adcock earned credits that he used for home maintenance. Cano, for her part, earned the credits that she used by assisting with recreational activities at a local nursing home. Although Fremont Time eventually disbanded as a formal organization, the friendship between Adcock and Cano continues and the journal expands each week.

The experience with Fremont Time was so positive that the State Division of Developmental Disabilities offered to support the Department of Neighborhoods to do similar work citywide. In 1997, we hired Carolyn Carlson to develop and manage a program called Involving All Neighbors. Carlson's first step was to organize the Action in Community Team, a committee of neighborhood and disability activists, to help shape and implement the program.

Involving All Neighbors launched a double outreach campaign that targeted neighborhood organizations on the one hand and, on the other, individuals with developmental disabilities and their families. Using workshops, the media, and the extensive networks of both the Department of Neighborhoods and the Action in Community Team, Carlson identified organizations and individuals wanting to participate. She worked in both directions. Sometimes she started with an individual and then identified an organization that was a good fit for his or her skills and interests. Other times, Carlson began with a neighborhood organization that she knew was seeking to be more inclusive and that she knew would then help reach out to include persons with disabilities. In every instance, the key was to find a "connector," someone who would serve as a link between the individual and the organization and take responsibility for making the relationship work.

One of the first individuals to get involved was Larry Moss, who became a leader in developing the transportation recommendations of the Capitol Hill Neighborhood Plan. Moss was a natural: because he is dependent on public transportation, he had extensive experience with bus riding and could speak as an expert about the various bus routes and how they could be improved. Moss also led a walking tour of the neighborhood, pointing out access problems not only for his crutches but for wheelchairs and baby strollers. Capitol Hill Community Council members came to value Moss's knowledge, his passion, and his dry sense of humor and soon elected him vice chair.

Moss and I were part of a Washington State delegation that was invited to Washington, D.C., for a meeting convened by the President's Council on Mental Retardation. I was grateful to have him as a traveling companion. Moss's keen sense of direction and his experience with public transit helped us make the best use of our time exploring the city. We especially enjoyed a performance of political satire by the Capitol Steps troupe. At the meeting, though, both of us took a strong dislike to the limiting and stigmatizing name of the sponsoring organization as it stared back at us from the large gold seal behind the podium: so, during a break in the meeting, Moss and I altered the seal to read President's Council on Full Inclusion.

Someone else who was involved from the start was Matthew Whittaker. Whittaker loves the outdoors and lives just four blocks from Ravenna Park. He joined the Ravenna Creek Alliance and learned how to remove the invasive plants that were threatening the creek. It wasn't long before he was organizing work parties and teaching others. Whittaker also came up with an ingenious idea for removing the pesky holly. At Christmas time, he recruits his friends and neighbors for a holly gathering party along the creek followed by a "Hollyday" lunch at his home. Whittaker and Moss are both members of the Action in Community Team and have made frequent presentations in Seattle and elsewhere on how to build inclusive organizations.

In West Seattle's Westwood neighborhood, it was the neighborhood council that took the initiative to be more inclusive. Susan Harmon, council chair and a member of the Action in Community Team, sought out people with developmental disabilities to get involved with her organization. When she visited the home of Ginger and Raymond Balch, she asked about the plaster of Paris clowns decorating their living room. The couple told Harmon how they had in the past enjoyed making crafts and also clowning—Raymond had been known as Raytoe the Clown, and Ginger had acted as his assistant—but with declining health and decreasing mobility, they had long since lost their connections to the West Seattle community. Harmon invited them to entertain the children at the upcoming Delridge Neighborhoods Festival. They were a big hit. Then she registered the Balches to participate in the Southwest Community Center's annual craft and plant sale. There they met a craft-loving neighbor who offered to drive them to additional community events. With each event, the network of friends expanded. The community benefit expanded as well. As Harmon put it, "Ginger and Raymond, just by being who they are, have opened doors for many of us in West Seattle."

One of the most fascinating examples of a neighborhood organization taking the lead in inclusion is a group entirely composed of people with developmental disabilities. The West Seattle chapter of People First

Susan Harmon accompanies Raytoe the Clown at the Delridge Neighborhoods Festival. Photograph by Carolyn Carlson.

decided to create a new park surrounding a local water tower. They found a meeting place in the neighborhood, posted notices, handed out fliers, and rang doorbells to encourage neighbors to help them design the park. The broad participation resulted in a creative design with something for everyone. Previously unused land was transformed into a wonderful park, and a previously invisible group, People First, became recognized by the West Seattle community as an asset.

Dozens of people with developmental disabilities have been involved in their communities through Involving All Neighbors. That involvement has not only enriched those individuals' lives, but it has enriched the organizations they have joined and has vividly demonstrated the value of being inclusive. In the process, the organizations have learned how to welcome and support a much wider variety of neighbors who are different from themselves in all sorts of ways.

The American Association on Mental Retardation recognized Involving All Neighbors with its Full Community Inclusion Award in 2000. The association noted that this was a unique program for local government and that the Department of Neighborhoods was ideally suited to making it a success.

Involving All Neighbors was heavily influenced by John McKnight and Jody Kretzmann, codirectors of the Asset-Based Community Development Institute at Northwestern University. McKnight and Kretzmann are critical of institutions, such as government and human service agencies, when these institutions keep marginalized populations dependent by focusing only on their needs. McKnight and Kretzmann encourage communities to be more self-sufficient by building on their assets, including the gifts that each person has to offer.

Like me, McKnight was trained in the Saul Alinsky school of community organizing: bringing people together around an issue in opposition to a common enemy, usually local government. Although McKnight retains the Alinsky premise that communities need to organize around issues, he helped me see that there are also other ways to bring people together. Starting where people are is an important principle of community organizing, and to do that you must recognize that many people are uncomfortable attending meetings while others are uncomfortable with conflict, both of which accompany most issue-based organizing.

McKnight told me about his friend who is a duck hunter. The friend has different kinds of calls for different kinds of ducks. Organizations, McKnight said, should do the same thing, adding that "too often, the only call that organizations use is the loon call, and then they wonder why only the loons turn out for meetings." For organizers, as for duck hunters, a variety of calls is essential. Some people will answer the call to rally around a particular issue. Some will turn out for work parties or to pitch in on a particular project in their neighborhood. Others will be attracted by a dance or a festival or by freshly baked brownies. The more calls an organization uses, the more broadly based its membership will be. And the more broadly based the membership, the more power the organization will have to address whatever issues matter most to its members.

SMALL SPARKS

Another key advisor on community organizing was Jeff Bercuvitz of Community Innovations in Vermont. We sought Bercuvitz's help to apply the lessons from Involving All Neighbors to other individuals who were not connected with their communities. Bercuvitz understood that, to start where people are, you may need to reach out to them where they live—literally where they live, on their own block. The closer an issue, project, or event is to a person's home, the more likely that person will be to participate. In addition, people tend to follow their personal passion, such as gardening, animals, or art. The likelihood of involvement gets even higher when the dimensions of that involvement are clearly defined as being manageable, in other words, when a limited commitment is required. Those were the ideas that ignited the Small Sparks program.

In 1998, extensive outreach brought twenty-eight formerly uninvolved neighbors to an all-day workshop facilitated by Bercuvitz. His enthusiasm was contagious and the Hershey's Kisses he likes to toss out every time an idea gets tossed out kept everyone attentive and energized. Bercuvitz had workshop participants identify "neighborhood treasures," whether that was a restaurant with especially delicious food, a gigantic cedar tree, or a long-time resident. He also got participants to identify their own skills and interests. In addition, Bercuvitz had people talk about "pockets of people" in their neighborhood, like the kids who play basketball at the park or a neighborhood walking group, and how to recruit them. Then each participant was asked to propose an activity that would build on these assets. Bercuvitz offered some tried and true maxims for people to keep in mind while developing their proposals: "Don't have a meeting when you can have a party," "Provide food and they will come," "If you get young people involved, their parents will come," and "Don't sit on your assets." By the end of the day, the participants had completed the one-page project applications and were eligible to be reimbursed for up to $250 for project-related expenses.

Ten projects resulted from that first workshop. The Small Sparks program expanded as neighborhood leaders were trained to recruit and coach additional workshop participants. Several months after each workshop, participants reconvened to share their stories and celebrate the collective impact that they had made.

There are now dozens of stories about Small Sparks projects. In one neighborhood, where fallen apples created a rodent problem each year, a woman organized her neighbors to make cider, using a press she had rented with Small Sparks money. Two men in Delridge helped their neighbors build birdhouses, more than thirty of which were installed in nearby Westcrest Park. In front of a youth center on Capitol Hill, neighbors joined street youth to create the Garden of Homeless Angels, a memorial to homeless youth who have died. The Magnolia Community Center was converted into a health club for a day as seniors were treated to live jazz, a healthful lunch, and spa services donated by massage, reflexology, cosmetology, naturopathy, and yoga experts. A young woman organized a language exchange with the Russian immigrants who live in her University District apartment building. Another woman and her son decorated a wagon that they pull through their Wedgwood neighborhood, providing a convenient way for neighbors to share their magazines with one another.

One memorable project focused on Beacon Tower, a high-rise for low-income seniors and people with disabilities on North Beacon Hill. Even though Beacon Tower is surrounded by single-family homes, most seniors who live there have been isolated: neighbors don't enter the locked building and few seniors venture out. A young neighbor who wanted to change that worked with Beacon Tower residents to plan an event that would bring together Tower and non-Tower neighbors: a paper airplane flying competition. Everyone in the neighborhood got an invitation to come out on a Saturday morning either to fly paper airplanes from the Tower's fifteenth floor or just to watch. Neighborhood businesses provided prizes for those whose airplanes went the farthest or hit a ten-foot bull's-eye. Tower residents treated their neighbors to homemade baked goods. Then everyone went outdoors together to pick up the paper airplanes that littered the neighborhood.

Not all of the groups that the Department of Neighborhoods has helped to organize are engaged in activities that are as innocuous as flying paper airplanes and picking up litter. Some do, in fact, beat up on city hall. What communities do with their organizations is up to them, but the Department of Neighborhoods looks for ways to help organizations partner with the city for their mutual benefit. The partnerships are often initiated at the Department's Neighborhood Service Centers.

3

CONNECTING COMMUNITIES

Neighborhood Service Centers and District Councils

The Department of Neighborhoods manages thirteen Neighborhood Service Centers that provide valuable connections for Seattle's communities. The centers and their staff connect individuals with community organizations that share their interests, and they facilitate connections between organizations. They also connect individuals and organizations to city programs and services, especially those of the Department of Neighborhoods. In many ways, the centers are the foundation of the department's work.

The foundation was laid in 1973 when the City of Seattle followed Boston's example by establishing Little City Halls in six distressed neighborhoods. Storefronts were rented to provide places where people could pay their public utility bills and take their problems and complaints. As employees of the Human Services Department, the Little City Hall staff also developed local food banks and transportation programs in the early 1980s.

The Little City Halls are now officially referred to as Neighborhood Service Centers. In 2002, ten of the thirteen centers were located in leased storefronts in neighborhood business districts and the others shared space with a community center, a fire station, and a police precinct. To enable even better coordination of services and one-stop service delivery, new branch libraries are being built with space to accommodate four of the existing centers.

Seattle's public utilities (electricity, water, sewage, and solid waste) fund Department of Neighborhoods staff, who work as customer service representatives at seven of the centers. Citizens make about 275,000 visits to the centers each year to pay their public utility bills. Although most utility customers pay by mail, the Neighborhood Service Centers are popular among people with limited incomes. Some need to pay in cash because they have no checking account. Others need to talk with a staff person about how they can avoid a utility shut-off or arrange for credit assistance. Low-income customers also visit to get health- and human-service referrals.

The seven payment sites collect about $35 million in utility bill payments annually. Because they are set up to handle money, these sites also accept fines for parking and traffic tickets, payments for transit passes and pet licenses, and applications for passports. Passport processing is a relatively new service and has attracted a broader range of customers to the centers. More than twelve thousand travelers a year use the Neighborhood Service Centers in order to avoid the long lines at the federal passport office downtown.

In recent years, the payment sites have been hosting municipal court magistrates. People with parking and traffic tickets can request hearings in their own neighborhood rather than having to go downtown and risk a second ticket. Most hearings on minor infractions are now conducted at Neighborhood Service Centers, one of many ways in which the centers are making it possible for citizens to avoid the traffic congestion downtown.

The Neighborhood Service Centers house other city employees as well. In 2002, several centers contained staff for the Neighborhood Matching Fund, neighborhood plan implementation, and other Department of Neighborhoods programs. Office of Housing staff helped people with limited incomes obtain free weatherization and home repair services. Five centers had full-time crime-prevention staff who organized and supported block-watch groups. Although there have been subsequent cutbacks in some of this co-located staff, most centers continue to accommodate police officers who drop in to conduct interviews, complete paperwork, make phone calls, and eat doughnuts. Employees from the Mayor's Office of Senior Citizens and the Office of Civil Rights maintain hours at some centers. Even elected officials schedule appointments with citizens at the centers. Citizens appreciate their improved access

The Columbia City Neighborhood Service Center brings city government to the people. Photograph by Ian Edelstein, City of Seattle; reprinted with permission.

to city employees, and city employees like the arrangement as well. While the public loves to hate the faceless bureaucracy, they usually have a high regard for the individual employees they come to know.

When citizens stop in at a Neighborhood Service Center, they can pick up a wide variety of written materials. They can learn about community organizations, projects, and events from local newspapers, newsletters, and fliers. Bus and ferry schedules are available. People can obtain applications for summer youth employment, community garden plots, and the Neighborhood Matching Fund, as well as forms for voter registration, business licenses, and vehicle collision reports. They can study building codes, environmental impact statements, neighborhood plans, employment bulletins, and other government documents. Brochure racks display information on a host of city programs and services.

Just about any other information pertaining to Seattle city government is available via computer. Each center has a direct connection to the city's extensive Public Access Network, which describes the programs, services, and policies of every department. Citizens can also use the computers to send their questions, concerns, or comments via e-mail to city staff and elected officials.

Neighborhood organizations make good use of the meeting rooms found in most centers. The meeting rooms are also used for free legal clinics offered by the King County Bar Association. No-cost tax assistance is available at some centers as well.

As popular as the Neighborhood Service Centers are with the general public, they are perhaps even more highly prized by the business associations in the neighborhoods where they are located. Several neighborhood chambers of commerce have their offices located in the centers. In some neighborhood business districts, it is the Neighborhood Service Center that is the "anchor business." The Greater University District Chamber of Commerce was so anxious to get its center to relocate to the heart of the business district that it arranged for comparable rent, paid for the tenant improvements and moving expenses, and provided free parking tokens to the customers.

COORDINATORS

The most cherished resource at any Neighborhood Service Center is its coordinator. These thirteen Department of Neighborhoods employees are the link between the community and city government. The coordinators sometimes refer to themselves as being overt double agents.

The coordinators know the city's (and often county- and state-level) programs and services and the people who can best deliver them. They help citizens and organizations find their way through the bureaucratic maze and get what they need. The coordinators are also intimately familiar with the community. They regularly attend the meetings of the many community organizations in their district. They know the community's schools, agencies, businesses, and places of worship.

The coordinators serve as consultants to the rest of city government. They prepare monthly reports about community concerns and continually update a list of community contacts; these are shared with department heads and elected officials. When a department has a program it wants to promote or an issue it wants to discuss with a neighborhood, its first stop is the coordinator. The coordinator can brief department staff on the neighborhood's hopes and concerns as they relate to that program or issue and advise staff on logistics such as which organizations and leaders they should contact, how to communicate with the larger community, and where to hold meetings.

The mayor and some city councilmembers call on the coordinators to arrange for regular neighborhood walking tours. The tours are an invaluable way for elected officials to stay in touch with the public. They provide a good opportunity for neighborhood leaders to call attention to local problems. Politicians become much more sympathetic to the need for sidewalks and drainage when they are wading through a rain-soaked street than when they are sitting through a dry presentation on infrastructure needs in the insulated comfort of city hall.

Perhaps the most important role of the coordinators is to bring together the various community interests. When I hired coordinators, I looked for people who were active volunteers, because I wanted them to have the credibility and empathy that would make them effective community facilitators. I tried to assign them to work in communities other than their own, however, so that they wouldn't be seen as leaders promoting their own interests. While every interest group in the community has its own agenda, the coordinators' agenda is to help all the community groups and encourage them to find common ground with one another. Consequently, the coordinators are uniquely trusted by the community leaders with whom they work.

DISTRICT COUNCILS

Historically, the coordinators focused on the distressed communities in the immediate vicinity of their Neighborhood Service Centers, but there were areas of Seattle that were far removed from any center. With the advent of the Neighborhood Planning and Assistance Program in 1988, the coordinators were expected to serve all of Seattle. Three additional centers were added to the existing nine so that there was a better distribution of coordinators throughout the city.

Neighborhood leaders worked with the Planning Commission to divide Seattle into twelve districts, each defining the area to be served by a Neighborhood Service Center. Each district was intended to include about forty thousand residents but, more important, it was supposed to encompass a common sense of community across neighborhoods. The boundaries for each district were supposed to respect existing neighborhood boundaries.

In Seattle, neighborhood boundaries are usually defined in the bylaws of each community council. Because these groups are independent, not only of city government but of one another, the composite boundaries are extremely messy. Numerous boundaries overlap and there are even neighborhoods within neighborhoods.

When neighborhood leaders came together to draw the district boundaries, the map they created reflected those overlaps. Notwithstanding city planners' fears that it would be difficult to get an accurate count of widgets per district if boundaries were allowed to overlap, neighborhood leaders insisted that the overlaps be retained. They wanted the city to respect how each neighborhood had identified itself and to understand that the overlapping boundaries documented areas of shared interest. Some district boundary overlaps have been negotiated away over time, but a few still remain.

More controversial was a provision of the Neighborhood Planning and Assistance Program stipulating that twelve district councils be established, each with one representative from each community council and neighborhood business organization in the district. Neighborhood leaders were suspicious that the district councils would take away power from their grassroots organizations. They were concerned lest community and government attention shift to the district councils, detracting from neighborhood groups and creating a layer of bureaucracy between them and city government.

Having observed district council systems in other cities and seen that government-sponsored entities could indeed undermine the existing organizations that belonged to the community, I sympathized with the communities' concerns. Some municipal governments, in the course of bestowing funding and authority on their district-level organizations, had also set boundaries for neighborhoods and standards for neighborhood organizations, determining which ones to recognize for membership at the district level. That system, while possibly making sense in a city lacking strong grassroots organizations, didn't seem like a good model for Seattle. Seattle had a long history of such organizations and more that were up-and-coming. The combination of controls on those grassroots organizations and special treatment for district organizations could conceivably reduce the power that neighborhoods already had. Government-sponsored groups are no substitute for the community's own organizations: the former tend to be farther removed from the people and are inherently dependent on city hall's political whims and budget fluctuations.

I believed that the strength of Seattle's neighborhood organizations was precisely in their independence from city hall. These organizations had survived for decades without funding from the city, and they had exercised considerable power. Their legitimacy and power came not from the city but from the people they represented: this was real power, dependent only on the degree of community support.

It seemed to me that district councils could make sense only if they contributed to the independent power of the neighborhood organizations. Mayor Royer and councilmember Street shared this belief, so district councils were granted no authority other than a role in rating Neighborhood Matching Fund projects. Unlike the grassroots organizations, the district councils cannot apply for project funding. The district councils serve primarily as a forum for neighborhood organizations to share information and ideas and, if the member groups so desire, to work together on common issues.

Staffed by the coordinator, a district council represents as few as eleven and as many as thirty-four local groups. Member groups are recognized by their peers, not by the city. The city does insist that both business and residential groups be included, but it is up to each district council to determine the standards whereby specific groups are admitted. Several district councils have elected to include other kinds of groups as well, such as parent/teacher associations and human-service providers, in order to ensure a broad representation of interests. Some district councils are more active than others. Most meet monthly and two meet quarterly. Every one of the district councils, however, has played an important role in building positive relationships among neighborhood groups.

Neighborhood groups' relationships with one another in 1988 were usually either nonexistent or contentious, especially between residential and business groups. Community councils, which were frequently at odds with their business neighbors over growth issues, were dubious about having neighborhood business organizations represented on the district councils. "Why should merchants get a second voice when they already have one as residents," it was argued, "and if they aren't Seattle residents, why should they have any voice at all?"

I got a good taste of this acrimony when I attended the founding meeting of the Capitol Hill District Council. The president of the Capitol Hill Community Council introduced herself and said, "I'm fairly new to the community council, but I know that we can't work with the chamber of commerce. We never have, and we never will." Those sentiments were echoed just as strongly by the new president of the Capitol Hill Chamber of Commerce. At that point, I was wondering why I had wanted this job.

After the other representatives had introduced themselves, people were asked to identify their group's top issues. When compiled, the lists on butcher paper revealed that the chamber and community council shared many priorities: public safety, traffic and parking, educational quality, and the health of the Broadway business district. While it was true that they had different perspectives on some of those priority issues, both groups realized over time that they could be more effective if they worked out their differences and developed consensus positions. From a place of consensus, the groups could approach the city as a united front rather than let the city make the compromises for them or use their differences as an excuse for inaction.

This organizational odd couple of Capitol Hill has made common cause in a number of instances over the years. When a series of hate crimes threatened Capitol Hill's gay and lesbian community, the groups jointly sponsored a public forum and posted a declaration of human rights in store windows. Together, they built a wheelchair-accessible playground for the many students with disabilities at Lowell Elementary School. They joined forces to oppose the construction of a television transmission tower in the neighborhood and they succeeded. The two groups worked together to develop Capitol Hill's neighborhood plan. And every year, the groups hold a banquet at which they honor both business and residential leaders.

The downtown neighborhood groups found it much easier to unite because they had an issue in common that demanded immediate attention: the Planning Commission and Seattle City Council had neglected to include them in the Neighborhood Planning and Assistance Program; no Downtown District or Downtown District Council had been envisioned.

Although the downtown neighbors were outraged at the time, this slight from city hall may have succeeded in accomplishing what nothing else could have accomplished in bringing together a number of disparate groups. These downtown groups ranged from the homeless of Pioneer Square to the wealthy condominium owners in the Denny Regrade, from the small-business owners in the International District to the movers and shakers of the Downtown Seattle Association. Together, they successfully demanded that the city hire a thirteenth coordinator and establish a thirteenth district council.

Following this quick victory, the Downtown District Council members tried to determine what it was that they had in common. It took very little discussion to realize that the greatest desire they had in common was for public restrooms. Every constituency needed them— homeless people, tourists, and shoppers alike. And everyone suffered when doorways and alleys had to substitute for restrooms.

The district council inventoried existing restrooms and in the resulting "Toilet Paper" identified where additional twenty-four-hour facilities were needed. As a result, the Department of Neighborhoods hired a public restroom coordinator whose business card identifies her job title as Head Honcho. Street signs now point people to public restrooms, facade-enclosed portable toilets provide some relief, and self-cleaning units have finally been ordered.

Thirteen years ago downtown was seen as a threat by neighborhood interests if it was seen at all. Neighborhood leaders who felt oppressed by downtown interests organized a successful initiative to cap the height of downtown office buildings. Now there is recognition that downtown is also made up of neighborhoods, and the tensions are much reduced. Downtown leaders have taken their place along with other neighborhood leaders. Jan Drago, the small-business owner who led the restroom campaign, was elected to the Seattle City Council. More surprising, Kate

Joncas, the director of the Downtown Seattle Association, was elected president of the City Neighborhood Council, the organization comprising representatives from all thirteen district councils.

While downtown was fighting to gain a district council, West Seattle was arguing to get rid of one. The Planning Commission had decided that the West Seattle peninsula, because of its size, was entitled to two districts. The proposed dividing line was 35th Avenue Southwest. I was called to a meeting by angry representatives from both halves of West Seattle. "How dare you divide us," they said. "We're one community." Although they argued for one district and one district council, they made it clear that they still expected two Neighborhood Service Centers, two coordinators, twice the representation on the City Neighborhood Council, and whatever else two districts would have entitled them to. I readily agreed.

Within a year, though, the representative of the area east of 35th Avenue Southwest had changed her mind. Vivian McLean was a longtime member of the Delridge Community Association, a small group valiantly trying to advocate for their large community. She complained that her part of West Seattle, the half with the greatest poverty, diversity, and neglect by the city, was getting short shrift on the district council. As the sole representative from Delridge, she was vastly outnumbered by more than a dozen representatives from the rest of West Seattle. McLean wanted to secede and form her own district council to give more attention to the unique issues of Delridge.

"You can't do that," I protested. "The whole purpose of district councils is to bring different neighborhood groups together. You need more than one group to form a district council." "How many more?" McLean replied.

Vivian McLean is a truly remarkable woman. She cares passionately about social justice, the environment, youth, and her community. She was a longtime activist in labor, her church, and her neighborhood. Now that she has retired as a teacher, she volunteers as a tutor and is involved in citywide neighborhood, environmental, and peace organizations. One day she might be clearing trash along Longfellow Creek and the next she could be demonstrating at the School of the Americas in Georgia.

Vivian McLean rose to my inadvertent challenge. Within two years, she had organized six new community councils and a Delridge District Council. She didn't stop there, though. She has now organized a total of thirteen community councils so that every neighborhood in Delridge is represented. She also cofounded the Delridge Neighborhoods Development Association, which recently built the community's first public library as part of a mixed-use development named, appropriately, Vivian McLean Place.

The other West Seattle groups weren't happy about this breakaway district council. They presented me with petitions signed by more than 1,200 residents demanding that I not divide West Seattle. The objections came too late: Delridge had already been organized. Tensions have dissipated with time, and the two district councils meet together periodically to work on common issues. Now, though, they are meeting as equals.

4

BUILDING COMMUNITY
The Neighborhood Matching Fund

The Neighborhood Matching Fund has been surprisingly successful at what it set out to do: build community, both physically and socially. Through the program, the city provides funding in exchange for the community's match of an equal value in cash, volunteer labor, or donated goods and services in support of citizen-initiated projects. From $150,000 in 1989, the program grew to $4.5 million by 2001, a year in which it supported more than four hundred neighborhood-based projects. Not only are the projects transforming the physical appearance of the neighborhoods, but they are building a stronger sense of community by involving thousands of people from all walks of life. The program has also yielded additional resources, numerous innovations, and new partnerships between communities and city government.

Over its first thirteen years, the Neighborhood Matching Fund backed more than two thousand projects. Community groups used the program to build new playgrounds at most city parks and public schools; create new parks; reforest open space; plant street trees; develop community gardens; restore streams and wetlands; create murals, banners, and sculpture; install kiosks; equip computer centers; renovate facilities; build traffic circles; pilot community school programs; document community histories; develop neighborhood plans; organize new groups; and much, much more. These projects are visible in every neighborhood of Seattle.

In 1991, the Neighborhood Matching Fund was recognized by the Ford Foundation and Kennedy School of Government at Harvard as one of the ten most innovative local government programs in the United

States. The program has, in turn, fostered many innovations of its own. To name just a few, the fund has been used to create a wheelchair-accessible playground (Alki), a drug-free zone (Garfield), and a community school (Powerful Schools); to conduct intergenerational oral history (African American community); to paint murals to combat graffiti (Central Neighborhood Association); to provide reforestation with native plants (College Street Ravine); to promote the reuse of rainwater (Cascade); to facilitate the "gray to green" conversion of asphalt to park (former Webster School); to restore a wetland to drain a ball field (Meadowbrook); and to create and install a troll to spark economic development (Fremont). All of these projects were firsts for Seattle. The community, which initiated them, tends to be more creative than the bureaucracy.

In Seattle, the bureaucracy has learned over time to accept, if not wholeheartedly embrace, community innovations. That certainly wasn't true initially. When I first talked with the director of the Department of Parks and Recreation about the Neighborhood Matching Fund, her reaction was, "We don't want people messing with our parks." I bit my tongue for a change and listened. She had legitimate concerns. "What about liability for volunteer work? Who will enforce our department's standards? Where will our department find time to be involved in these projects? How will the improvements be maintained?"

We worked with Parks and Recreation and other city departments to figure out how to make the program work for them. We found a carrier for liability insurance. We agreed not to fund any project unless it had been reviewed and approved by the appropriate departments. The Neighborhood Matching Fund pays for two positions in the Parks Department and one in Transportation, providing guidance to the community and a liaison to other staff members in those departments. All project contracts include provisions for ongoing maintenance by the community, the appropriate department, or both.

Now Parks and Recreation is one of the Neighborhood Matching Fund's strongest advocates. Rather than saying no to community ideas that Parks and Recreation can't afford, the fund gives the department a way to meet the community halfway. An idea with a lot of community support provides an opportunity for the Parks Department to work

International District activists cre-
ated sixteen dragon poles welcom-
ing visitors to their neighborhood.
Photograph by Jim Diers.

collaboratively with the community. If the community support doesn't materialize, the department isn't seen as the obstacle. The Department of Parks and Recreation has developed many more positive relationships with communities as a result of the Matching Fund. Parks has also found that community members take care of the projects they create, often utilizing the department's Adopt-a-Park program. Seattle Transportation, the Arts Commission, Seattle Public Utilities, and the Seattle School District have had similar conversion experiences.

Of course, a big incentive for departmental participation is the additional resources. Besides the $23 million contributed by the Neighborhood Matching Fund between 1989 and 2001, the community has generated more than $30 million in matching resources. Every dollar invested by the program in recent years has leveraged an average of $1.60 in community match.

A large portion of the match has come in the form of volunteer labor. At last count, more than a million volunteer hours had been contributed

Miller Park residents celebrate the completion of Ron K. Bills Fountain, a project of their own creation. Photograph by Ian Edelstein, City of Seattle; reprinted with permission.

to projects. Many hours of skilled labor have also been donated. Together, these skilled and unskilled volunteers account for tens of thousands of people, many of whom have become involved in their community and with their local government for the first time.

The Neighborhood Matching Fund gives people an opportunity to get involved without necessarily going to meetings. Although meetings have been the traditional form of community involvement, many people are meeting-averse. Too often, meetings seem to result in nothing but more meetings. The Matching Fund enables people to make a short-term commitment in support of a time-limited project. They know their involvement is making a difference, and they see results. In the process, they develop relationships that may lead to their participating in other projects or maybe even attending meetings. The Matching Fund has proven to be an effective tool for increasing the membership of existing community organizations.

The creation of new organizations is another result of Neighborhood Matching Fund projects. Many neighborhood arts, educational, environmental, and historical groups as well as ethnic organizations trace their origins to a Matching Fund project. There are now more ways than ever before to be involved in community life.

The Neighborhood Matching Fund empowers communities in other ways as well. Not only do citizens initiate, manage, and implement projects; it is community organizations that make the major funding decisions. In the first year, when $150,000 was available, the money was divided equally among Seattle's thirteen districts. Each district council was responsible for deciding which projects to fund with its $11,538. Some districts didn't have enough proposals to use all of the money, while other districts had many more solid proposals than they could support.

The next year, neighborhood leaders decided to have only one city-wide pot of money so that they could compare proposals across districts and fund those that demonstrated the greatest need and the most involvement, no matter their location. Each district council rated the applications from its district and appointed a representative to a City-wide Review Team that rated all of the applications. The combined district and citywide scores were used by the City Neighborhood Council to recommend which projects to fund.

That year, 1990, $1.5 million was available to support projects requesting $2.3 million. The City Neighborhood Council members, however, recommended only $1.1 million in awards, because they thought that the remainder of the proposals were of insufficiently good quality. Can you imagine elected officials leaving money unallocated when they had constituents asking for it? But the citizen review process is not subject to politics, and for that reason it is highly respected by politicians (and by other funders who readily contribute to projects that have the Matching Fund seal of approval). Both the mayor and city council have consistently upheld the recommendations of the City Neighborhood Council. Not only does the citizen review process have great integrity, it has this additional benefit: with citizens making the recommendations, politicians don't get blamed for rejecting proposals; elected officials are identified with only the funded projects and can take their bows at the continuous stream of groundbreaking and ribbon-cutting ceremonies.

Besides making funding recommendations, the City Neighborhood Council was also empowered to develop the overall guidelines for the Neighborhood Matching Fund. The City Neighborhood Council was ably and invaluably assisted in the effort by the longtime managers of the program, Bernie Matsuno and Rebecca Sadinsky. Although the guidelines continue to be refined, the basic eligibility and selection criteria that were developed in 1988 are still in place today.

ELIGIBILITY AND SELECTION CRITERIA

The City Neighborhood Council developed two sets of criteria for the Neighborhood Matching Fund. The first criteria define what kinds of organizations can apply and what kinds of projects are eligible for funding. The second criteria are used to rate eligible applications as the basis for funding decisions.

Neighborhood leaders developed the eligibility criteria with several goals in mind. They wanted to use the Neighborhood Matching Fund as a tool to create and strengthen grassroots organizations. They wanted project funding to be as accessible as possible, especially for people who had been marginalized, and, at the same time, they wanted to avoid making community organizations dependent on government funding.

Eligible applicants were defined as those organizations that had open membership and that were democratically governed and neighborhood based. This definition includes community councils and neighborhood business organizations and also neighborhood-based groups with specific focuses such as arts, education, environment, history, public safety, or recreation. An organization need not be incorporated in order to apply to the fund. In fact, neighbors who come together for the sole purpose of undertaking a project can be eligible. Agencies and religious, partisan, and fraternal organizations cannot apply.

In 1990, eligibility was extended to organizations representing communities of color. This was done in recognition that people of color tend to be underrepresented in neighborhood organizations. The eligibility extension was also premised on an understanding that, because of language and cultural differences, Seattle's growing immigrant and refugee population tended to identify more with ethnic groups than with neighborhoods.

Eligible projects, no matter what, must be neighborhood specific. They must also be time limited, and their outcome must benefit the public. Phased projects are allowed, but each phase must stand on its own, because there is no assurance of future funding. In fact, ongoing programs are not eligible. The Neighborhood Matching Fund cannot be used for basic operating costs such as staff salaries or rent. The purpose of that restriction is to keep the fund flexible so that it can support new projects each year. More important, the fund aims to empower organizations to be self-sufficient. Projects are an ideal way for communities to build their organization's membership and expertise. Direct funding of organizations, in contrast, could foster a dependence on city government, leaving organizations vulnerable when elected officials are faced with tight budgets or hostile constituencies.

One exception to the prohibition against funding programs is pilot projects that involve and benefit both a public school and its neighbors. Eligibility was extended to such pilot projects in an attempt to restore the connection that neighborhoods and schools had lost during the busing program. This public school partnership category has made it possible for neighborhoods to initiate community school programs, computer centers, tutoring, and other programs. Even with this exception, however, project requirements support the larger goal of fostering independence: the application must include a plan for self-sufficiency, because the Neighborhood Matching Fund will not support a second year of operations.

Another key eligibility criterion, as indicated by the fund's name, is that a proposal must include matching community resources. The value of the match for neighborhood improvement projects must at least equal the amount of funding requested. Here again, an exception to the rule was made to accommodate community realities: only half as much match is required for organizing low-income communities and for planning, since it is more difficult to generate local contributions for such projects.

The match can be in the form of cash, volunteer labor, or donated goods and services. At the time of this writing, unskilled labor is valued at $12 an hour, and skilled services, if shown to be needed, are counted at the market value. At least 25 percent of the match must come from the community that benefits from the project. The match must be documented in the project application, including pledges of time, materials, and cash.

Eligible applications are rated against eight selection criteria developed by the City Neighborhood Council. Each criterion is weighted with its own range of possible points. About half of the points are awarded for standard grant writing criteria such as demonstrated need for the project, cost-effectiveness, and readiness to proceed.

The remainder of the points focus on citizen participation. What are the opportunities for self-help? To what extent does the project include diverse participants? How secure is the community's match?

Taken all together, these criteria help ensure that funding and empowerment are being directed where they are most needed. When the Neighborhood Matching Fund began, there was a concern that affluent neighborhoods would be in the best position to come up with a match and that people not represented by strong community councils would be left behind. This has proven not to be the case, however: the provisions that count volunteer labor as a highly valued match, that make organizing an eligible project in low-income neighborhoods, that include organizations for people of color as eligible applicants, and that emphasize need and diversity as selection criteria have helped to ensure that a disproportionately large share of the funding has gone to low-income communities.

FUNDING AND CONTRACTING

The Neighborhood Matching Fund grew dramatically during its first thirteen years. In 1989, the first year awards were made, forty projects received a total of $150,000. In 2001, $4.5 million was disbursed across more than four hundred projects. The first major funding increase came in the program's second year, when it grew tenfold to $1.5 million. The funding stayed at that level for eight years until Paul Schell took office as mayor in 1998. He proceeded to make good on his campaign pledge to triple the Matching Fund. Aided by Richard Conlin of the Seattle City Council, Schell gained approval for emergency legislation that doubled the fund to $3 million his first year in office. By 2001, he had succeeded in increasing the fund to the full $4.5 million.

Had candidate Schell consulted me about his plans, I would have tried to talk him into a more modest expansion of the program. I shared the skepticism of some city councilmembers who couldn't imagine communities coming up with enough good projects and accompanying matches to warrant such a large increase in funding. We feared there would be more funding than requests, removing the competition that had made the rating process work so well.

But Schell proved to be right. The number of applications skyrocketed so that the program was more competitive than ever, with about one-third of the proposals having to be turned down. Much of the increased demand was due to the recent neighborhood planning program that had involved thirty thousand people in generating more than four thousand ideas for improving their neighborhoods. Many of those ideas translated readily into Matching Fund projects, and there was, moreover, a newly involved constituency to carry out the projects. Equally a factor in the increased demand was the fact that the Matching Fund had evolved over time to better accommodate projects of all sizes.

A demand for projects of all sizes was evident early on. In the first citywide competition for funding in 1990, two very different applications came from the same community. A proposal from the Rainier Vista Community Council requested $100,000 to renovate the play field in their public housing community. The nearby Hillman City Action Group applied for $100 to install a community notice board outside a corner grocery store. These disparate proposals had to use identical application forms and go through the same six-month review and approval process. The Southeast District Council and the Citywide Review Team found it difficult to compare and rate two proposals when one was a thousand times bigger than the other.

To accommodate the wide variance in project scope, the City Neighborhood Council adjusted the program the following year by dividing the Matching Fund into two main components. Proposals requesting $3,000 or less for projects that could be completed within six months were eligible for the Small and Simple Projects Fund. Projects needing more than $3,000 and up to a year to complete would apply to the Large Projects Fund.

Applications for large projects are now accepted twice a year. Applicants must submit a letter of intent describing their proposed project. The letters are reviewed by the Department of Neighborhoods and any other agencies that would be involved in the project. Staff advise the potential applicant on how to shape the final application so that it can be supported by the city and be as competitive as possible when rated by the district council and Citywide Review Team.

Prior to the doubling of the Neighborhood Matching Fund to $3 million in 1998, no project had ever been awarded more than $100,000. Rating points were automatically deducted for every increment of $50,000 requested in order to spread the money further by creating a preference for midsize projects. Those penalty points were eliminated in 1998 and, as a result, projects requesting as much as $300,000 have been funded.

Another change in 1998 was that the maximum request to the Small and Simple Projects Fund was increased to $10,000, making it even more popular than it had been before. Citizens like the relatively easy application and contracting forms. They also appreciate having three times as many opportunities to apply: applications to the Small and Simple Projects Fund are accepted every other month, in contrast to the Large Projects Fund's twice-a-year deadlines.

Perhaps the most popular feature of the Small and Simple Projects Fund is that funding decisions are made within one month of the application deadline. Decisions can be made so quickly compared to the six months for large project applications because the Small and Simple Projects Fund process requires no pre-application and because the proposals are rated by the Department of Neighborhoods rather than through the citizen review process. As a result of this shortened time line, the Small and Simple Projects Fund is seen by the community as a kind of "opportunity fund," with communities able to secure funding within weeks of envisioning a project.

The proliferation of smaller projects did have one regrettable outcome that we had failed to foresee: it created a severe strain on staff. These small projects require much more staff time per dollar awarded than do the larger projects. To make more time available for small projects, the department had to drop another component of the Neighborhood Matching Fund, the Youth Fund.

The Youth Fund, and the Anti-Violence Fund before it, was managed by a half-time staff person, but these Matching Fund components were even more time consuming per dollar awarded, because projects were limited to $1,000. Only youth-led groups were eligible to apply, so a separate outreach effort was required to contact and help organize that constituency. Additional time was needed as well to staff a separate review team composed entirely of youth, including my daughter, Kati. I hated to have to terminate the Youth Fund, because it had proved so effective in empowering youth and had resulted in some innovative and much-needed projects, such as a gay/lesbian youth magazine, peer mediation, an anti-violence rap video, a multicultural mural, and park beautification. Youth-led groups can and do apply to the Small and Simple Projects Fund, but the process is less accessible than was that of the Youth Fund.

The department has maintained the other components of the Neighborhood Matching Fund that it has developed over the years. There is the Outreach Fund, to which community organizations can apply once a year, at any time, for up to $750. The money must be used for a campaign to recruit new members. Expenses might include constructing a sandwich board to advertise meetings, printing enough copies of one issue of the organization's newsletter to distribute to the entire neighborhood, or staging a community picnic to attract new members.

A more recent development was the establishment of a Tree Fund. Planting trees along streets and in parks has always been a popular type of project. Even with the pared-down Small and Simple Projects Fund, groups must fill out the application, shop for the best tree value, haul the trees to the site, and document the match. With the Tree Fund, a person simply recruits five or more neighbors who would like to plant trees in front of their houses or in a nearby park, and notifies the Department of Neighborhoods. An arborist from the Transportation Department (for street trees) or Parks and Recreation (for trees in a park) then helps the neighborhood select appropriate trees and specific locations.

Seward Park neighbors work together to plant a street tree. Photograph by Ian Edelstein, City of Seattle; reprinted with permission.

The Department of Neighborhoods compiles all of the orders each spring and fall and solicits bids from local nurseries. Not only are large cost savings realized, but the nursery delivers all of the trees. Each tree-planting group must send one representative to a half-day workshop on planting and caring for trees, but no documentation of match is required. Experience has shown that planning, along with planting and caring for trees, has a value roughly equivalent to the cost of the trees. To cite the figures for just one season, in October 2001 the Tree Fund was used by 134 neighborhood groups to plant 4,400 trees throughout Seattle.

All of these components of the Neighborhood Matching Fund supported a total of 418 projects in 2001: 30 large projects received a total of $2.58 million, 156 small projects received $1.03 million, 57 outreach projects received $24,000, and 175 tree projects cost $136,000. The city's $3.77 million investment leveraged a community match of $5.62 million for a total project value of $9.39 million. The administrative costs, including ten staff, totaled $730,000, less than 8 percent of the cost of the projects.

All but $220,000 of the $4.5 million Neighborhood Matching Fund comes from the city's General Fund. The remainder of the money is from the federal Community Development Block Grant. That arrangement affords the Matching Fund more flexibility because, unlike money from the General Fund, Block Grant money can be used for improvements to private property as long as the improvements have public benefit. Block Grant dollars are restricted to low-income neighborhoods, and the federal funding requires much more paperwork, so the General Fund is the source most useful to most applicants.

Not many of the organizations applying to the Neighborhood Matching Fund have much capacity for handling money. Most have no staff and have never undertaken a project prior to applying for Matching Fund money. Few have sought tax-exempt status from the Internal Revenue Service, and many are not even incorporated. The typical applicant has little or no money in the bank. Washington State's constitution prohibits the city from lending public credit, so the Department of Neighborhoods can reimburse only for expenses incurred. Consequently, most neighborhood groups have had to partner with a nonprofit organization willing to serve as fiscal sponsor.

A contract for each project is signed by the Department of Neighborhoods, the community organization, and the fiscal sponsor. The contract describes the project, lists the time line and budget to complete the work, and identifies what contributions are to be made by the city and what by the community. The contract also includes provisions for competitive bidding, equal opportunity, liability insurance, and ongoing maintenance.

SHARING STORIES

Prior to the Neighborhood Matching Fund, most grassroots organizations focused their energies on fighting projects that they did not want to see implemented in their neighborhoods. We realized that organizations would need a great deal of encouragement to change their focus to projects that they did want. They would also need assistance in selecting, planning, and implementing those projects.

We knew that there was a fair amount of community interest in building new playgrounds, so the first year the Neighborhood Matching Fund was available we sponsored a workshop on playgrounds. The workshop was presented by experts from the Department of Parks and Recreation, the Seattle School District, and the University of Washington. The training was well received and resulted in several new playgrounds.

We repeated the workshop the following year, but this time our panel of presenters featured the neighborhood volunteers who had managed playground projects. The volunteers were able to talk frankly and from personal experience about how to work with bureaucrats, mobilize the community, create a design in keeping with a neighborhood's special needs and character, and raise funds. They also conducted a tour of the playgrounds that they had built. This workshop was far more effective than the first year's because it provided neighborhood volunteers with the information they most needed. More important, the workshop provided inspiration: seeing the impressive projects completed by their peers gave these newer activists confidence that they too could succeed.

The department has used this peer assistance approach ever since, for projects of all kinds. Every year, it hosts an Ideas Fair at which about twenty model projects are featured. Each project sponsor is assigned a table and encouraged to create a display. Community members can arrive at any time during the half-day event and visit the displays that interest them most. Project sponsors are on hand to answer questions and offer encouragement. This has proven to be an ideal way to introduce people to new project ideas and to acquaint them with peers who can serve as mentors.

Various other methods for sharing stories have been used as well. Workshops on specific types of projects, including tours of a sampling of completed and in-progress projects, continue to prove educational and inspiring—and also fun. The coverage of projects in local newspapers and newsletters enlarges the way people think about what they can do in their own communities. The department also produced a series of six "Help Yourself!" booklets describing some of the ways in which people have used the Matching Fund to create projects related to cultural heritage, the environment, neighborhood organizing, playgrounds, public art, and public school partnerships: each booklet tells the story of a handful of projects and then, so readers can act on their inspiration, lists dozens of community contacts, individuals and agencies, who can be consulted. Following are some of my favorite stories, including a few details and a number of stories that never made it into the booklets.

Fremont Troll

Several months after Norm Rice took office as mayor in 1990, I made a presentation to his cabinet regarding the Neighborhood Matching Fund. I was eager to gain the new mayor's support for the program, so I talked about the many ways in which the Matching Fund was improving Seattle's public schools, something I knew Rice felt passionately about. I thought I was making a good impression when Engineering Director Gary Zarker piped up, "Hey, Diers, why don't you tell the mayor about the troll you funded?" The mayor sounded incredulous: "A troll?" Even before he added, "We can't afford to maintain our streets. Don't tell me we're spending public funds on a troll," I was wondering if the troll, one of our first projects, might also be one of our last.

My predicament had started innocently enough. In 1989, the Fremont Community Council had been granted $3,833 to build a pocket park on either side of the Aurora Bridge where the bridge connected with the neighborhood. This state-owned property had long been a place of overgrown weeds and unsightly litter. Converting this problem property into Bridge Park seemed like a good idea.

> **Project: Sculpture at Bridge Park**
> **Sponsor: Fremont Arts Council**
> **Location: Aurora Avenue North and North 36th Street**
> **Year awarded: 1989**
> **Amount awarded: $22,400**
> **Amount leveraged: $27,325**
> **Year completed: 1991**

When the street-level park was completed, the community's attention turned to the area beneath the bridge. This site had become a magnet for illegal dumping and encampments, and the community wanted to turn it into an extension of Bridge Park. Community members sought help from the Fremont Arts Council, the group that had given the neighborhood its reputation for funky art.

The Arts Council saw the area under the bridge as the perfect place for a large sculpture. Arts Council members noted that the support columns for the high bridge created an imposing, cathedral-like atmosphere. They named the space the Hall of Giants and applied to the Neighborhood Matching Fund for $22,400 to create the appropriate sculpture.

I was uncomfortable with the application because it nowhere specified what kind of sculpture would be created or who would create it. The proposal said that the artist would be selected by the community after the project had been funded. Notwithstanding my discomfort with this to-be-determined approach, the City Neighborhood Council approved the project.

The Arts Council advertised a call for artists, inviting them to submit entries. The finalist entries included larger-than-life construction workers as a tribute to the people who built the bridge, a gigantic throne for the Hall of Giants, and a troll. Models of the three sculptures were displayed at the Fremont Fair and the fair's 100,000 visitors were invited to vote for their favorite. As I wandered around the fair, I kept circling back to the booth, voting repeatedly for the construction workers sculpture: of the options offered, it seemed the least objectionable.

Crime never pays, and the troll won anyway. It was my worst fear come true. Regina Hackett, the art critic for the *Seattle Post-Intelligencer*, was incensed. In her July 27, 1990, column she wrote: "If 'the people' want bad art by majority vote, should public money be used to provide it? . . . Visual art benefits all, but there is such a thing as being a specialist in making and choosing it. Undemocratic as it sounds, not all opinions are created equal." She used a subsequent column to berate the troll as a "cement monstrosity" and "cutesy banality."

Hackett's comments roused the Fremont community to rally behind the troll. When I visited the neighborhood one day, there were ten-foot-long footprints up and down the streets. People I asked said that the troll had been walking through. The community quickly raised funds to fulfill its match requirement.

When the community failed to convince the Seattle Arts Commis-

Elected by popular vote, the Fremont Troll rules. Photograph by Ian Edelstein, City of Seattle; reprinted with permission.

sion to include the troll in its collection, the community went instead to the Board of Public Works. *Fremont Troll* was the first public artwork ever approved by that body. Architect Steve Badanes and his fellow Jersey Devils went to work building the troll, incorporating an actual Volkswagen bug that the troll clutches in one hand as if he has just snatched it from the bridge overhead.

There was some vandalism early on, but the community responded by organizing a troll patrol. Patrol members installed lighting under the bridge and walked the neighborhood at night to ensure that the troll was safe. The community also started a tradition of celebrating Trolloween on October 31, with a huge procession beginning at the troll. The troll has developed a far-flung reputation, bringing tourists and their money to Fremont.

And Regina Hackett? In the *P-I*'s July 11, 1991, issue, she admitted that it was "time to eat troll. As trolls go," she conceded, "this one sports rugged, sullen grace and monstrously droll charm. The people voted for it, and now they're voting with their feet. The former eyesore is now a landmark, a Fremont classic."

Murals for All

Scores of murals have been created throughout Seattle with support from the Neighborhood Matching Fund. Murals can be created by people from all walks of life, and they lend themselves to showcasing the history, values, and characteristics of a neighborhood. Moreover, murals have proven to be an effective tool for promoting economic development, motivating youth, and combating graffiti.

The first set of fund-sponsored murals was proposed by the Central Neighborhood Association. Community members wanted to do something about the growing graffiti problem in their neighborhood, so they organized to paint out the graffiti as soon as it appeared. Just to keep buildings looking the same, however, proved to be a lot of work. Members of the neighborhood association came up with a more proactive strategy. If they involved neighborhood youth in painting murals on walls that had been frequent targets of graffiti, they reasoned, perhaps the graffiti artists would respect their fellow artists and leave those walls alone.

The Central Neighborhood Association worked with Black Muslim artists and students from Garfield High School to paint a series of murals. The murals not only proved to be an effective anti-graffiti strategy, but they also brought together an amazingly diverse community. The dedication of the murals was hosted by a Jewish women's auxiliary, held in a Lutheran church, and attended by Black Muslims, along with the diverse students and neighborhood association members, all of whom were celebrating together.

Graffiti was less of a problem in West Seattle's Alaska Junction, but Earl Cruzen thought that a collection of historical murals could draw shoppers to this struggling business district. He organized three groups of volunteers: the first group researched the history of West Seattle and determined the subject for each mural, a group of local artists then issued a call for artists and served as the jury to select finalists from among the artists who applied from all over the world, and a third group was needed to serve as the hospitality committee. Hospitality committee volunteers hosted the artists in their homes and escorted them to local events so that they could be a part of community life. They also helped attach plywood to the buildings to serve as a work surface, build scaffolding, and procure supplies. Some volunteers even got to help with the actual painting. The final result is a remarkable collection of eleven large murals depicting the history of the neighborhood and known collectively as *Murals of West Seattle*.

> **Project: Murals of West Seattle**
> **Sponsor: Junction Development Committee**
> **Location: Vicinity of California Avenue Southwest and**
> **Southwest Alaska Street**
> **Years awarded: 1989 and 1992**
> **Amount awarded: $54,393**
> **Amount leveraged: $61,048**
> **Year completed: 1993**

One of those murals, showing the public market that used to be located across the street from Ken Olsen's drugstore, was painted on the back of the drugstore, facing the parking lot and adjacent arterial. Olsen told me that customers so much enjoyed watching the mural in progress that he never heard any complaints about how long it took him to fill their prescriptions. On the other hand, his store was the site of more than one argument between customers trying to recall the original color of the market so that they could advise the artist.

As is typical of Matching Fund projects citywide, West Seattle community members take great pride in what they have created, and they watch out for and maintain the murals. A local artist told me that he had just started touching up a mural one day when a police officer stopped him: a concerned neighbor had tipped him off that someone was defacing the mural.

Mike Peringer, director of the SODO (South of Downtown) Business Association, understood the potential for murals to spruce up and enliven his industrial neighborhood. He especially wanted to improve the appearance of 5th Avenue South: a primary route for buses coming into downtown from the south, the street was flanked on both sides by the graffiti-covered backs of warehouses. Peringer wanted to create a more inviting gateway to Seattle, and he also wanted to make it a better environment for the neighborhood's workers. His idea was to paint murals the length of the two-mile corridor and to build a walking path and pocket parks so that the workers as well as the commuters could enjoy them.

> *Project: SODO Urban Art Corridor*
> *Sponsor: SODO Business Association*
> *Location: 5th Avenue South between South Spokane*
> *Street and Royal Brougham Way South*
> *Years awarded: 1997 and 1998*
> *Amount awarded: $146,289*
> *Amount leveraged: $174,739*
> *Year completed: 1999*

Peringer wanted to get even more out of the project, though, so he decided to hire at-risk youth, most of whom are on probation. He teams the youth with artist-mentors to create vivid and sometimes astonishing murals on a grand scale. Forty such murals now line the corridor, improving the ride for fifteen thousand commuters a day. In a spin-off project, the youth have been painting murals on plywood panels to surround construction sites. These murals have given Seattle some beautiful artwork while providing the means for youth to learn life skills as well as artistic skills.

Several Matching Fund murals have a labor theme. The King County Labor Council and Judkins Park Community Council worked together to create a mural with several panels that depict the local history of African American migration, work, protest, and community. A mural in the International District's historic Eastern Hotel depicts the labor history of the Filipino community as portrayed in the writings of Carlos Bulosan, who once lived in the hotel. In Belltown, Latino day workers wait for jobs in front of a large mural showing organized farm workers marching toward Seattle.

Now in Seattle, murals are everywhere. Artists have worked with students in schools to paint murals on dozens of bus shelters. The undersides of bridges in Ballard, Fremont, Green Lake, and South Park are covered with murals. One of my favorite mural projects was created by Coyote Junior High students, who transformed the bunkerlike Medgar Evers swimming pool: the mosaic mural on the front depicts the life of

Artists of all sizes paint a mural on the wall of the North 57th Street Underpass leading to the zoo. Photograph by Lise Ward.

Medgar Evers, and the mosaics on the side have water themes. Another favorite is the block-long mural on the side of a Rainier Valley dairy plant: it celebrates the community's multicultural heritage and includes, top and center, a portrait of Jimi Hendrix.

Reforestation with Native Plants

Charlie Chong's house overlooks the College Street Ravine, five wooded acres in West Seattle. Although much of the ravine had been privately owned, Chong and his neighbors assumed that the land was undevelopable because of the steep slopes. Then one day a backhoe arrived to clear sites for five new houses. Believing that development was likely to undermine the stability of the hillside and threaten the ecological health of the ravine, the neighbors organized as the Friends of the College Street Ravine and successfully lobbied the city to purchase the property with its share of the county's open space bond money.

Once the neighbors were focused on the ravine, they realized that it was in poor health. Long ago, the creek had been filled in and the forest of cedar, hemlock, and Douglas fir logged. English ivy had taken over more than a third of the property, crowding out the ferns, salal, and other native plants. Even before the backhoe had left deep holes in the hillside, the ravine was covered with debris from illegal dumping.

The Friends of the College Street Ravine organized a symposium to discuss the best approach for restoration. Should they simply fill in the holes, clean up the trash, and maintain the existing vegetation, or was there a better solution? What would be the best habitat for the birds and other wildlife? They invited naturalists, nursery owners, landscape architects, biologists, arborists, and bird and other wildlife experts to present and debate different strategies for restoring the ravine. After much discussion and continuing self-education, the group decided to remove the invasive vegetation and reforest with native plants.

None of the open space bond money could be used to improve the property, so the Friends of College Street Ravine turned to the Neighborhood Matching Fund. The fund paid for new plants, landscape cosultants, equipment rental, and waste disposal. Most of the match came in the form of the volunteer labor involved in removing the invasive plants and planting native varieties of trees, shrubs, and groundcover. It was a huge job for the group's forty-three members, but they persevered. Even so, it will be a long time before the wooded area is fully restored to its natural state. "Some of us on this project will not live to see the trees mature," said Chong, "but we're planting them for future generations."

Project: College Street Ravine Restoration
Sponsor: Friends of College Street Ravine
Location: Southwest College Street between 47th and
51st Avenues Southwest
Year awarded: 1989
Amount awarded: $6,600
Amount leveraged: $10,960
Year completed: 1991

The project has created benefits beyond the improvements, both present and future, to the ravine's ecology; you might say it has improved the neighborhood's sociology as well. Neighbors, previously separated by the ravine, now know one another as friends. The Friends of the College Street Ravine expanded to become the Admiral Community Council.

Blair and Dow Constantine, neighbors who volunteered while students at the University of Washington, were lastingly influenced by the project. Blair is now a landscape architect specializing in native plants. Dow's advocacy for the project took him into politics, first as a state legislator and now as a county councilmember. Chong formally went into politics as well, making a successful bid for election to the Seattle City Council.

College Street Ravine leaders developed expertise that helped shape the city's Critical Areas Ordinance. They also continue to advise neighborhood groups all over the city who have been inspired by the example of the College Street Ravine and are undertaking or thinking about undertaking their own reforestation projects. Chong refers to this as the rippling effect of the Neighborhood Matching Fund.

Recently, the ripples were felt in the Madrona neighborhood. Working with local schoolchildren, neighbors reforested Madrona Woods with

The Madrona Woods Waterfall is the neighbors' alternative to a drainage pipe. Photograph by John Toczek, City of Seattle; reprinted with permission.

native plants. They also built a trail and stairway down the steep slope. During one of their work parties, they dug up a pipe that was channeling spring water from the hillside into the storm drain below. Rather than replace the pipe, the group installed boulders where the pipe had been to create a spectacular urban waterfall. I used to drive past the spot every day on my way to work, and I'm probably not the only motorist who nearly drove off the road at the startling sight of a waterfall that seemed suddenly to appear from nowhere.

Another reforestation project that involved schoolchildren was the Harrison Greenbelt. Members of the Madison Valley Community Council wanted the students to get as much as possible out of their volunteer work on that reforestation project, so they used the Neighborhood Matching Fund to publish a textbook. *City Woods* relates the ecological history of the neighborhood and identifies native plants. The book also describes the social history of the community from the Native Americans to the African American migration to the present. Jerry Sussman, who authored the textbook, volunteers at Martin Luther King Elementary School, where he teaches a class on that subject.

Diamonds in the Rough

Floyd Schmoe, a lifelong naturalist and peace activist, worked as a ranger on Mount Rainier and a volunteer in the reconstruction of Hiroshima. At the age of 95, Schmoe decided to combine his passions by building a "peace park" across the street from the University Friends meeting hall. The site he selected was a strip of Transportation Department property between 40th Street and the Burke-Gilman Trail below. Overgrown with brambles and littered with trash, it was one of many Transportation Department properties that was not maintained because it served no transportation purpose.

Schmoe and his Quaker friends, many of them his contemporaries, cleared and regraded the land. They planted trees and shrubs native to Japan and the Pacific Northwest. The centerpiece of the park is a life-size statue of Sadako Sasaki, the girl who folded paper cranes as she was dying of leukemia caused by the bombing of Hiroshima, and through whom the paper crane has become an international symbol of peace. Now children from all over make pilgrimages to Seattle Peace Park as well as to Hiroshima's Peace Park, draping chains of origami cranes over Sadako and also, without knowing it, paying tribute to Schmoe, who recently died at the age of 105.

Project: Seattle Peace Park
Sponsor: Seattle Peace Park Associates
Location: Northeast 40th Street
and 9th Avenue Northeast
Year awarded: 1990
Amount awarded: $2,809
Amount leveraged: $3,063
Year completed: 1990

Weather Watch is one of many waterfront parks that have been created out of formerly neglected street ends. Photograph by Jim Diers.

The end of West Seattle's Carroll Street was another useless property as far as the Transportation Department was concerned. Although it had served as a ferry landing until the 1940s, it no longer supported any kind of transportation. Thus ignored, this piece of Puget Sound shoreline had become an overgrown, litter-strewn eyesore.

Among the many neighbors who saw this property as a problem, one neighbor, an artist named Lezlie Jane, saw the property's potential. She organized her neighbors to clear the litter and invasive vegetation from the site. Jane researched plants that thrived in a salt-water environment and she and her neighbors landscaped the property accordingly.

Then it was time to create and install the artwork that Jane had envisioned for Weather Watch Park. The park's focus is a sculpture topped by a weather vane of Canada geese; the base displays photographic images of different types of clouds to help visitors predict the weather headed for Seattle (as if we didn't know). The sculpture is the centerpiece of a patio of five hundred bricks engraved with weather-related phrases and the names of area residents, including early settlers. A curved, concrete bench is inlaid with a bronze relief map of the Olympic mountains so that visitors can identify the peaks (whether or not they are visible). Jane and her neighbors have been too busy to spend much time sitting on the bench, though. They went on to create Constellation Marine Reserve and Cormorant Cove, two more shoreline parks that combine whimsical, educational artwork with beautiful, site-appropriate landscaping.

> *Project: West Seattle Weather Watch*
> *Sponsor: Alki Community Council*
> *Location: Southwest Carroll Street and Beach Drive Southwest*
> *Year awarded: 1989*
> *Amount awarded: $20,865*
> *Amount leveraged: $23,985*
> *Year completed: 1990*

Karen Daubert wanted to do something similar with Lake Washington street ends in her Leschi neighborhood. The problem was that the affluent homeowners on either side of these street ends had expropriated them over time by growing hedges or building fences in order to deny public access. Lacking any public outcry, city officials had turned a blind eye to this practice in some cases and charged a token street-use fee in others.

Daubert's determination to regain public access inspired the Leschi Community Council to apply to the Neighborhood Matching Fund to create four street-end parks. Despite opposition from adjacent property owners, the community council accomplished what the city would not do on its own. Volunteers removed the obstructions, installed plantings and a bench in each park, and erected signs proclaiming public access. These pocket parks have proven to be urban oases that can be enjoyed by people, usually one or two at a time, seeking a quiet and beautiful spot; they have not attracted the beer drinking crowds that the immediate neighbors had feared. In fact, some of those same neighbors now help with the parks' ongoing maintenance.

Daubert continued her commitment by founding and chairing the Friends of Street Ends. The organization advocates for public access at all of Seattle's 134 street ends and provides technical assistance to neighborhood organizations that want to develop them as pocket parks. More than a dozen street-end parks have been established on Lake Washington, Lake Union, Puget Sound, and the Duwamish River using the Neighborhood Matching Fund.

> *Project: String of Pearls*
> *Sponsor: Leschi Improvement Council*
> *Location: South King, Dearborn, Norman,*
> *and Charles Streets at Lakeside Avenue South*
> *Year awarded: 1995*
> *Amount awarded: $3,448*
> *Amount leveraged: $5,178*
> *Year completed: 1996*

The Neighborhood Matching Fund was used to convert yet another Transportation Department property into a park, this one in the heart of the Phinney business district. Where Phinney Avenue curves left as it goes north past the Phinney Neighborhood Center, the right-hand lane continued straight to the intersection, where it was separated from the main arterial by an asphalt traffic triangle. The community had for some time been wanting to create a kind of town square for Phinney. When someone pointed out the spot's potential—it was a middle-school student who actually thought of the idea—the community got permission to tear up the traffic triangle and the lane between it and the sidewalk in order to create a park. The Matching Fund paid for the landscaping, pavers, cement benches, and pedestrian lighting, and the community supplied the volunteer labor to shape these elements into a green and inviting gathering place.

The park was just being completed when terrorists attacked New York City and Washington, D.C., on September 11, 2001, and it became the place where the community came together to grieve and support one another. An old tower for air raid sirens looms over the park on one side. On the other side is a bench inscribed with Mahatma Gandhi's words, "You must be the change you want to see in the world." The park, which (like most places in Seattle) is located next to a coffee shop, has continued to be the place where neighbors meet. The student who had been looking out the window of that coffee shop when she came up with the idea for the project also came up with a name for it, which was adopted and has proven apt: Heart of Phinney.

> *Project: Heart of Phinney Park*
> *Sponsor: Friends of Heart of Phinney Park*
> *Location: Phinney Avenue North and North 67th Street*
> *Years awarded: 1998 and 2001*
> *Amount awarded: $75,000*
> *Amount leveraged: $100,540*
> *Year completed: 2001*

Garfield Drug-Free Zone

Seattle has established drug-free zones surrounding all the city's schools and parks, doubling the penalty for drug dealing in those areas. But the first and most effective drug-free zone was initiated by the Garfield

Garfield residents organize a drug-free zone to take back their neighborhood. Photographer unknown.

Community Council. Led by George Stewart, the council responded to a rising tide of crack cocaine dealing and the attendant violence by drawing a line around their entire neighborhood and declaring it a drug-free zone. They vowed that drugs would not be tolerated in their community, and they backed up their words with large Friday night marches through the streets of Garfield. In the course of the marches they would stop to stand in silent vigil in front of the houses where dealers lived. The community's courageous stand had an impact: open drug dealing nearly disappeared. The declaration of the zone and the ensuing marches and vigils also proved to be an effective way to build a stronger sense of community and to reaffirm pride in the Garfield neighborhood.

Project: Garfield Drug-Free Zone
Sponsor: Inner City Drug Abuse Task Force
Location: Garfield Neighborhood
Year awarded: 1989
Amount awarded: $20,000
Amount leveraged: $17,810
Year completed: 1990

Operation Homestead

One fall day, I was sitting in my office downtown when I heard a familiar kind of commotion outside. Jumping up to look out the window, I was excited to see the street below filled with marching demonstrators. Then I took a closer look and swallowed hard. The protesters' banner read "Operation Homestead." I recognized it as the name of the homeless organizing project we had recently funded.

The group proceeded up the street, where they broke into the abandoned Pacific Hotel and announced their plans to remain as squatters. They wanted to draw attention to the fact that, while Seattle's streets were full of homeless persons, here was a perfectly habitable building lying empty. The demonstrators stayed until the police evicted them six days later. In the meantime, the *Seattle Times* covered the story with a large photograph and article on the front page of the local news section. The headline read: "City Gives Money to Occupation Forces."

I received some angry phone calls, including one from a city councilmember demanding to know why we were funding lawbreakers. Fortunately, Mayor Rice backed me. Although he wasn't happy about the occupation, he understood that empowering communities is not without its risks. We bought some peace by agreeing to add a provision to future Matching Fund contracts specifying that city money cannot be used for illegal activities.

The Pacific Hotel was subsequently reopened as low-income housing. Operation Homestead provided training to the tenants in management. The Department of Neighborhoods helped obtain the historic tax cred-

Supporters cheer the squatters who have occupied the former Pacific Hotel. Photograph by Benjamin Benschneider, Seattle Times; reprinted with permission.

its that made the project possible. How's that for full service?—helping with everything from the takeover to the financing.

> *Project: Homestead Organizing Project*
> *Sponsor: Homestead Organizing Project*
> *Location: Downtown*
> *Year awarded: 1993*
> *Amount awarded: $26,590*
> *Amount leveraged: $20,270*
> *Year completed: 1994*

The Neighborhood Matching Fund has also been used for other, less controversial projects to benefit community members who are homeless. An outreach van for services to the homeless was purchased by the

Pioneer Square Community Council with Matching Fund money. The Denny Regrade Community Council sponsored the development of a gallery for homeless artists. On Capitol Hill, the chamber of commerce launched a voucher program as a constructive alternative to panhandling.

ReTree Ballard

Dervilla Gowan loved trees. Ballard, where she lived, had very few trees in its parks (there were very few parks as well) or on its streets. So Gowan started a campaign called ReTree Ballard. She posted fliers in local stores and made a plea in the *Ballard News* for people who shared her passion for trees to join her. Her goal was to identify someone on every block in the neighborhood. If they didn't come to her, she knocked on doors to recruit block leaders. Gowan finally enlisted thirty-six block leaders and gave them each a packet titled "How to successfully mobilize your block to do a street tree planting." The block leaders agreed to attend a training session on how to plant and care for trees and to ask their neighbors to sign forms pledging to help. Gowan submitted the pledge forms as part of ReTree Ballard's application to the Neighborhood Matching Fund.

One spring Saturday, trucks drove into the neighborhood to deliver trees to each block. The block leaders gathered their neighbors and taught them how to plant the trees. By the end of that day, 1,080 people had helped plant 1,080 trees up and down the streets of Ballard. Everyone marveled at what a big difference they had made in so little time by working together. The community was ready for more projects, and they had developed a network that would make more projects possible.

> *Project: ReTree Ballard*
> *Sponsor: Central Ballard Community Council*
> *Location: Ballard neighborhood*
> *Year awarded: 1994*
> *Amount awarded: $39,242*
> *Amount leveraged: $76,150*
> *Year completed: 1994*

Groundswell Northwest

With less park space than any other neighborhood in the city except for downtown, Ballard lacked what makes Seattle the Emerald City. Their new street trees inspired neighborhood leaders to continue working to make Ballard as green as possible. They banded together to form Groundswell Northwest, with a mission to acquire and improve public lands for public purposes.

The first step was to inventory open space. With support from the Neighborhood Matching Fund to pay for a project coordinator, volunteers walked the neighborhood in search of vacant lots and potentially vacant lots that could be converted into public spaces. Ballard is so developed, though, that neighbors had to be creative in their inventorying and include the possible reuse of land with abandoned railroad tracks and street ends. They even identified the installation of boulevards and traffic circles as a strategy for gaining open space. When the inventory was complete, neighbors attended a community workshop at which they placed possible property acquisitions in order of priority. Groundswell Northwest then began lobbying the city to purchase those properties at the top of the list.

Groundswell's first improvement project required no acquisition at all, however. The project's focus was a large sea of asphalt that adjoined the former Webster Elementary School. What had once been a playground for the school and the neighborhood was now a parking lot for the Nordic Heritage Museum, which leased the eighty-year-old building from the Seattle School District.

Across the street lived Lillian Riley, a former teacher and the first president of Groundswell Northwest. Riley negotiated with the museum, the Seattle School District, and the Department of Parks to reduce the size of the parking lot, arguing that it was much larger than what the museum needed most of the time. With an award from the Neighborhood Matching Fund, Groundswell hired a landscape architect to work with all of the parties in redesigning the space to optimize its use. The museum agreed to make one far corner of the parking lot available for a playground. The other far corner could accommodate basketball courts and a ball wall, and it would be separated from the parking lot by bollards that could be removed when extra parking space was needed for special events.

What was especially innovative within this creative solution was the design of the new playground. Rather than simply reinstall play equipment on the asphalt, the community chose to remove the asphalt and to plant grass, shrubs, and trees. Webster Park was Seattle's first "gray to green" project, and now similar parks are replacing asphalt playgrounds at schools throughout the city. This is a multifaceted strategy: not only does it create additional green space without the cost of land acquisition; it also provides a natural and more effective solution to drainage problems.

There are many other compelling elements to Webster Park. Local artists created a gigantic sundial and walls with Viking ships in relief. Bronze leaves are embedded in the park's curving pathways. And the play equipment itself—of which there is plenty in Webster Park—looks much better in the context of its green surroundings than it would have on the asphalt.

Project: Webster Playground Project
Sponsor: Groundswell Northwest
Location: 3014 Northwest 67th Street
Year awarded: 1995
Amount awarded: $49,872
Amount leveraged: $319,207
Year completed: 1996

Groundswell's next project, led by Dave Boyd, was in the Crown Hill neighborhood. The organization had successfully lobbied the city to purchase a half-acre lot in the heart of the business district. The property, on which sat a dilapidated house inhabited by transients and surrounded by blackberry bushes and trash, needed a great deal of work. The city, however, had no money to improve the site.

Using the Neighborhood Matching Fund, Groundswell cleared the property and worked with a landscape architect to design Baker Park. Volunteers constructed an arbor entrance and planted butterfly and shade gardens. The landscape architect and volunteers also designed and

Neighbors recognized the potential value of a dead tree in a blighted lot. Photograph by Ian Edelstein, City of Seattle; reprinted with permission.

created a meadow play area complete with two giant boulders for climbing. The community tried to save the property's beautiful old trees, which had been part of the Baker family's Depression-era nursery, but one of them, a large monkey puzzle tree, succumbed to old age. Rather than remove the dead tree, Groundswell contracted with a Haida Indian to carve a totem pole. Topped by a raven, the totem features a variety of animals traditional to Haida folklore, including a bear carrying a frog in its mouth, symbolizing the return of nature to Crown Hill.

Project: Baker Park
Sponsor: Whittier Heights Community Council
Location: 8347 14th Avenue Northwest
Year awarded: 1995
Amount awarded: $81,587
Amount leveraged: $82,287
Year completed: 1997

Groundswell has used the Matching Fund to develop additional open space projects of all sorts in the greater Ballard community. One of them,

Crown Hill Glen, uses a natural area, paths, and stairways to tie together four blocks that are at different elevations, connecting neighbors with the environment and with one another. Two other projects, Greg's Garden and Thyme Patch Park, offer gardening opportunities in parklike settings. Soundview Playground and Salmon Bay Sportsfields provide space for active recreation, as does Ballard Skate Park, built by young neighbors and their parents. And as befits a neighborhood noted for its ties to the fishing industry, there's even a project for Ballard's fish: Groundswell has acquired and is restoring the last wooded stretch of shoreline on Salmon Bay, critical salmon habitat in the estuary linking the Cedar River watershed with Puget Sound.

African American Oral History

Communities throughout Seattle, both geographic, like the Alki neighborhood, and ethnic, like the Vietnamese community, have used the Neighborhood Matching Fund to conduct oral history projects. The first such project, by and about the African American community, was one of the richest, because the elders were interviewed by teenagers. All of the interviews were documented on video and KOMO television edited them to produce a half-hour program. I attended a reception and screening of the video in the community room of the Central Area Motivation Program, the project's sponsor. Many community members had come to watch the video and to honor the fifteen youth and fifty elders who had made it possible. Like everyone there, I was impressed by how well the video succeeded in portraying the history of Seattle's African American community.

What I found even more impressive, though, was hearing and seeing how the project had changed the attitudes of the youth and the elders toward one another. The youth no longer thought of the elders as boring and irrelevant. They had learned how the elders had fought for civil rights to make life better for successive generations; they enjoyed the elders' senses of humor and gained a better appreciation for their values. The elders, in turn, gained experience that allowed them to go beyond the stereotypes of youth offered in the media: these youth were eager to learn and they had conducted the interviews with skill and poise. It was a joy to be at that reception and see the two generations interact with such mutual respect.

The value of the project may be best summarized by interviewer Makeeba Pate: "My favorite question was, 'What gives you hope for the future?' To hear them say that it was the young people. . . . Before, I thought they'd given up on the young people. I feel responsible to keep doing good in school, because people are behind me. For them to think that things would get better made me hopeful, too."

Project: Central Area Senior Community History Project
Sponsor: Central Area Motivation Program
Location: Central Area
Year awarded: 1992
Amount awarded: $49,721
Amount leveraged: $53,148
Year completed: 1993

Kids Building Boats

Among Neighborhood Matching Fund projects, it's not unique to be unique. But one of the most extraordinary projects in that category was undertaken by one of Seattle's most extraordinary neighborhood organizations, the Floating Homes Association. This organization of houseboat dwellers partnered with Alternative Elementary School #1 to pilot the Kids Building Boats program. Volunteers worked with at-risk youth, teaching them boat-building skills at the Center for Wooden Boats on Lake Union. The students learned mathematics, woodworking, and maritime history while building ten 10-foot sailboats. Sailing and water safety lessons followed. The students formed the first public school yacht club in the Pacific Northwest and elected a female African American as commodore, another first. Not to be outdone, the South Park community used the Matching Fund to teach their youth how to rebuild and race a hydroplane.

Project: Building Boats for Kids and Communities
Sponsor: Floating Homes Association
Location: 1010 Valley
Year awarded: 1990
Amount awarded: $5,000
Amount leveraged: $8,400
Year completed: 1992

Meadowbrook and Pritchard Wetlands

Ball fields always seem in short supply in Seattle, so the Meadowbrook neighborhood was eager to get more use out of theirs. The problem was that their ball field was unusable much of the year due to poor drainage. The community submitted a letter of intent to apply for a project to drain the ball field.

The Department of Parks reviewed the proposal and came back to the community with bad news: it would be a very involved and expensive project. The grass would need to be dug up, the field regraded, drainage pipe installed, and sod replaced. And, after several hundred thousand dollars' worth of work, the field would be much drier but would look much the same.

It was not an inspiring prospect, and regardless of inspiration, the community realized that they could not possibly raise that much in matching funds. Then the idea for an alternative project presented itself. From talking with longtime residents, Meadowbrook volunteers realized that the reason the field was always wet was that the site had originally been a wetland. The city, when creating the ball field, had simply excavated soil from the adjacent hillside and covered the wetland. When Janine VanSanden learned the origin of the problem, she imagined turning the problem into a solution: Why not restore the portion of the wetland at the base of the hill?

Despite the Parks Department's initial resistance to this unconventional proposal, VanSanden persevered. She organized her neighbors to dig a deep trench along the side of the ball field and create a berm. The creek reappeared. The community created two ponds along the course of the creek and planted vegetation native to local wetlands. Soon, wildlife returned: frogs, songbirds, and even great blue herons. Volunteers built a bridge across the creek, connecting the trail on each side. Today, Meadowbrook Wetland serves as a wonderful amenity for the community and as an environmental learning center for neighboring Nathan Hale High School. And, yes, the wetland serves to drain the ball field. As for VanSanden, she is now a valued employee of the Parks Department.

Project: Meadowbrook Wetlands Restoration
Sponsor: Meadowbrook Advisory Council
Location: 10750 30th Avenue Northeast
Year awarded: 1992
Amount awarded: $31,160
Amount leveraged: $37,915
Year completed: 1993

Meanwhile, in Southeast Seattle, Lisa Merki was determined to liberate a 4.5-acre wetland from the barbed wire fence surrounding it. Although adjacent to beautiful Pritchard Beach on Lake Washington, this wetland had been subjected to years of dumping and the unchecked growth of invasive plants. It had become a blighted area from which the public needed to be protected.

The city tried to talk Merki out of her plan to restore the wetland. It seemed like a project much too ambitious for a group of volunteers. But Merki held her ground. She was determined to reclaim the unused, uncared-for, and unsightly property as a critical ecological niche, a neighborhood connector, and an educational resource for nearby schools.

After successfully applying to the Neighborhood Matching Fund, the Friends of Pritchard Beach paid to have the land cleared and recontoured. Merki brought students to the site from neighboring Rainier Beach High School, South Shore Middle School, and Dunlap Elementary. The students worked with neighborhood volunteers to plant thousands of native shrubs and trees. Community members built a boardwalk across the

Young people played a key role in restoring the Pritchard Beach Wetland. Photograph by Ian Edelstein, City of Seattle; reprinted with permission.

property, connecting the landlocked neighborhood with Lake Washington. They also constructed an amphitheater overlooking a large pond to serve as an outdoor classroom. Students can now sit there and observe muskrats, red-winged blackbirds, and a wide variety of waterfowl. When my daughter worked at the nearby community center, the kids' favorite field trip was to walk over to the wetland and search for creatures in the pond.

> *Project: The Wetland at Pritchard Beach Park*
> *Sponsor: The Friends of Pritchard Beach Park*
> *Location: 5500 South Gratten Street*
> *Years awarded: 1998 and 1999*
> *Amount awarded: $184,589*
> *Amount leveraged: $558,450*
> *Year completed: 2000*

Carkeek's Salmon Playground

In 1979, Nancy Malmgren started working with her neighbors in North-west Seattle to enhance the Pipers Creek watershed. They educated the community about the environmental consequences of dumping motor oil down storm drains and of using fertilizers and pesticides on lawns and gardens. They lobbied the city and county to improve the drainage and sewage systems. After the Neighborhood Matching Fund was created, the group used it for several projects to control erosion and improve wildlife habitat along the creek by removing invasive vegetation and reforesting with native plants. Most of the creek restoration work occurred in Carkeek Park, a large forested area where Pipers Creek flows into Puget Sound. The group's goal was to make Pipers Creek so hospitable that, after many decades' absence, salmon would return to Seattle to spawn.

One November day in 1993, I got a phone call from Malmgren. Out of breath with excitement, she announced "They're back!" I raced to Carkeek Park, where I joined dozens of other celebrants to welcome home the salmon. Their struggle upstream to spawn was an incredible sight.

To ensure that the salmon keep returning in ever larger numbers, the community has taken on additional projects with the support of the Neighborhood Matching Fund. Several miles from Carkeek Park, in the Greenwood business district, the community contracted with artists to etch salmon into the sidewalk leading from the storm drains and to install metal salmon leaping out of the top of the nearby bus shelters to remind people that the headwaters of Pipers Creek are buried below. Volunteers are currently expanding and upgrading an education center in the park, using green technology. Meanwhile, regular weeding, planting, and trail-building parties continue and, every November, the salmon return.

Terry Walsh wanted to make Carkeek Park attractive to more than just salmon. She had in mind the many children who live near the park. Walsh organized her neighbors and brought them together with landscape architect John Barker to design a playground. When one child sug-

Salmon have returned to Carkeek Park (right) . . .

. . . and so have the children (below).

Photographs by Ian Edelstein, City of Seattle; reprinted with permission.

gested that the playground have a salmon theme, everyone got excited and the creative juices started to flow.

The signature piece of the playground is a slide: a nineteen-foot-long concrete salmon sculpture built by a local artist. To play on it, children (or, for that matter, adults) climb the stairs that lead to the salmon's mouth, dive in and slide out the tail to land in a sea of foam rubber. Children can also follow a winding path through the wooded hillside that takes them into a cave, over fallen trees, and through a hollow log, an obstacle course intended to give them a sense of the struggle that salmon undergo in their return to Seattle. The playground was landscaped with native plants and with driftwood. Among the play elements are ceramic tide pools and a spring ride in the shape of a sea lion.

Project: Carkeek Park Play Area Improvement Project
Sponsor: Carkeek Park Advisory Council
Location: 950 Northwest Carkeek Park Road
Years awarded: 1994 and 1995
Amount awarded: $96,375
Amount leveraged: $256,329
Year completed: 1997

Carkeek Park is just one of the new generation of innovative playgrounds being developed through the Neighborhood Matching Fund. Fifteen years ago, one playground looked pretty much like any other. Not anymore. Each of the more than one hundred school and park playgrounds that have been built by local communities reflects the unique character of the neighborhood where it is located. Seattle's first wheelchair-accessible playground was built by the Alki community, because they wanted to make sure that their youth with disabilities could enjoy it. The park next to the historic fire station that houses the Central Area Motivation Program is equipped with a fire engine–shaped climbing structure and spring rides designed as dalmations. Near Lake Union, the playground of Eastlake's Rogers Park features a play structure in the shape of a seaplane. Another distinguishing feature of these community-designed playgrounds is that virtually every one incorporates the work of local artists, most of whom are children.

Eritrean Community Center

The Eritreans in Seattle, like most immigrants and refugees, understand the importance of community. They know that their individual welfare depends on their supporting one another. Although many Eritreans work at low-wage jobs and must work more than one job in order to make ends meet, they always find a way to contribute to their mutual assistance association.

By pooling their savings, members of Seattle's Eritrean community were able to purchase a large piece of property in Rainier Valley, including a rundown house. Association members used their spare time to renovate the house to serve as a community center. They bought sewing machines and taught themselves how to make clothing and household items at the community center. They purchased used computers and learned how to operate them at the center. Most important, they remodeled the basement to include a large kitchen and dining area so that they could prepare traditional meals and eat together. The space was also used for music and dance lessons and for performances so that they could maintain their culture in that way as well. They did all of this with their own time and money, asking nothing from foundations or government agencies.

Very quickly, however, the mutual assistance association outgrew the house and the members made plans to build a large new community center on adjacent property. They decided to apply to the Neighborhood Matching Fund for help. Matching Fund guidelines stipulate that at least 25 percent of a project's match must come from the community itself. That seemed like a tall order for this community of recent immigrants. But they knew the crucial importance of community and the need for a place where they could all come together. So the mutual assistance association asked its three hundred members for money to match the dollars it was requesting from the city. Within a week of putting out the call, members had contributed $30,000. The $75,777 awarded from the Matching Fund enabled the association to leverage another $1 million from foundation and government sources. When the new center was dedicated, hundreds of celebrants, many dressed in traditional white silk gowns, packed the 4,700-square-foot building. They

Eritreans celebrate the opening of their community center. Photograph by Bradley Enghaus, Pacific Publishing; reprinted with permission.

were proud of what they had accomplished and excited about their new center's potential to foster an even stronger sense of community. Asmellash Ghebremedhin put it well when he told the *Seattle Times* (June 14, 2003), "The community is something like home."

> **Project: Eritrean Community Center**
> **Sponsor: Eritrean Association in Greater Seattle**
> **Location: 1528 Valentine Place South**
> **Year awarded: 2000**
> **Amount awarded: $75,777**
> **Amount leveraged: $1,000,000**
> **Year completed: 2003**

5

CULTIVATING COMMUNITY

The P-Patch Program

F ounded in 1973, P-Patch was one of the first community organic gardening programs in the nation. Other cities have replicated the program and called their gardens pea patches. They didn't realize that Seattle's *P* stands for *Picardo*, the family that owned the truck farm that became the site of the first community garden.

I like to think that the *P* also stands for *people*, because people is what community gardening is all about. More than five thousand people cultivate plots of ground in Seattle's P-Patch gardens, which give people an opportunity to work together as a community and to contribute to the larger community. "Flowers grow in flower gardens and vegetables grow in vegetable gardens," we say, "and community grows in community gardens."

Seattle's program continues to be the largest municipally managed community gardening program in the United States. In 2002, there were sixty-two gardens throughout Seattle, and additional gardens were being built at the rate of four per year. The program's seventeen acres support about two thousand garden plots that range from one hundred to four hundred square feet.

The program is managed by a small staff of five in the Department of Neighborhoods, while the gardeners themselves provide most of the resources. Gardeners pay annual fees of $24 to $58, depending on the size of the garden, to help cover basic costs such as rototilling, tools, water, and fertilizer. All of the P-Patch gardens have been built by the gardeners, usually with support from the Neighborhood Matching

Fund. One or more gardeners volunteer as the site coordinator at each P-Patch, working with staff to assign plots; organize orientations, work parties, and other gatherings; resolve problems; and identify recipients of the dreaded "weedy garden" postcards that warn gardeners that they will lose their plot if it is not better maintained. All gardeners are required to volunteer at least eight hours a year for the benefit of the P-Patch Program as a whole, but many volunteer much more time. Most of the super volunteers belong to the five-hundred–member Friends of P-Patch, a nonprofit organization established in 1979 to advocate for and help manage the program.

Although their flowers and fresh produce may be the most tangible benefit for the individual gardeners, the P-Patch Program serves Seattle's larger community in four important ways. First are the environmental benefits. The sixty-two gardens provide important open space in most neighborhoods and require no outside maintenance. The gardens attract birds, bees, butterflies, and other wildlife. Master gardeners and master composters use the gardens to educate the larger community about good environmental practices.

Second, the P-Patch Program builds a strong sense of community. As the gardeners work together to build and maintain their P-Patch, they develop close ties to one another. The Friends of P-Patch group brings these different communities together for citywide gatherings, including a series of progressive potlucks and the annual Day of Giving, the Great Tomato Taste-Off, and the Harvest Banquet.

Third, the gardens serve as community centers for the surrounding neighborhoods. All of the gardens are open to the public, with signs posted welcoming visitors. The gardens' common areas have play structures, picnic tables, benches, art, or other features designed to draw the community into the garden. Gardeners organize concerts, barbecues, art shows, plant sales, and other public events in their P-Patch that also strengthen the sense of community.

Promoting social equity is a fourth community benefit of the P-Patch Program. A Gardenship Fund managed by the Friends of P-Patch ensures that everyone has access to the program whether or not they can pay the annual fee. Approximately 25 percent of the gardeners have incomes below the federal poverty level, and 11 percent rely on food bank assistance.

Youth haul compost to create a garden of their own at New Holly. Photographer unknown.

Besides putting food (and flowers) on their own tables, P-Patch gardeners also feed others—many others. Each year, gardeners contribute eight to ten tons of organic produce to food banks through Lettuce Link, another program established by the Friends of P-Patch.

The P-Patch Program provides access to gardens for a variety of special needs populations and, in so doing, raises the larger community's awareness of these often overlooked neighbors. Sixteen gardens have raised beds designed to be accessible to people with limited mobility. Garden plots and programming specifically for children are included in fifteen of the P-Patches; University Heights and Marra Farm P-Patches provide plots for homeless youth. Eleven human service agencies have garden plots maintained by their clients.

Although African Americans are underrepresented in the P-Patch Program, about one-third of P-Patch gardeners are persons of color. Southeast Asians and East Africans, who account for about 20 percent of all gardeners, are the populations best served by the program. These relatively recent immigrants, many of them refugees, typically have agricultural backgrounds, so the opportunity to stay connected to the land

Customers meet the gardeners to pick up their weekly supply of fresh produce at the Rainier Vista market garden. Photographer unknown.

is especially—many would say critically—important. The P-Patch Program enables these transplanted people to grow food indigenous to their cultures and to rebuild a sense of community in their new, sometimes extremely foreign country.

Although gardens for Laotian refugees were among the first P-Patch sites built in the 1970s, most of the outreach to the Southeast Asian and East African communities has been accomplished through Cultivating Communities, a program founded by the Friends of P-Patch in 1995. With Cultivating Communities, P-Patch partnered with the Seattle Housing Authority to establish community gardens for public housing residents. For decades, Seattle's four large public housing developments were euphemistically called "garden communities," but there weren't any actual gardens until P-Patch got involved.

Today, there are seventeen gardens that are used exclusively by public housing residents, and virtually all of the gardeners are from Southeast Asia and East Africa. My favorite is the Most Abundant Garden, enclosed by a beautiful bamboo fence and gate made by the gardeners using traditional techniques. Three of the gardens were built and are being tended by youth. Three others are market gardens that enable public housing residents to make some extra income and enable outside customers to make cross-cultural connections as they learn how to use the "foreign" herbs and vegetables they purchase through annual subscriptions costing $350. The groundbreaking success of Cultivating Communities was recognized by the federal department of Housing and Urban Development with a Best of the Best Award in 2000.

Although Cultivating Communities has worked with increasing success to get the gardens to be self-managed, the program continues to be relatively staff intensive. Two P-Patch staff, several volunteer and paid interpreters, and a few VISTA volunteers have been needed because of the necessity for more extensive outreach, the indispensability of communication in numerous languages, the added complexity of market gardens, and the extra work involved in building so many new gardens.

Gardens are being added outside of public housing as well, thanks to a five-year strategic plan for the P-Patch program approved by the Seattle City Council in 2000. Although the plan addresses a range of issues, such as outreach to diverse communities and food security, what emerged as the plan's top priority was the development of additional gardens. Several factors made expansion paramount. First, plans recently adopted by city council call for the P-Patch Program to grow with Seattle's population. Seattle's Comprehensive Plan, adopted in 1994, includes the goal of one community garden for every 2,500 households in densely populated neighborhoods. Of the thirty-seven neighborhood plans approved between 1998 and 1999, twenty call for at least one additional garden. Development pressures, meanwhile, have resulted in the loss of some leased garden sites and have put more in jeopardy. Finally, the waiting list for P-Patch plots has grown: depending on the time of year, there are four hundred to eight hundred households waiting to be assigned a garden plot.

The P-Patch strategic plan commits to a net increase of twenty gardens over five years. To accomplish that goal, the plan specifies that new gardens should be under public ownership; existing public properties are preferred for budgetary reasons. So far, the program is on track to meet its goal. Despite the loss of two leased gardens, a net increase of eight gardens was achieved in the two years following the plan's approval by city council. Seven additional gardens are under construction. The sixty-two gardens include only ten leased sites. Of the rest, twenty-nine are owned by the city (fifteen by the Parks Department, six by Transportation, four by City Light, three by Neighborhoods, and one by Facilities), fifteen by the Seattle Housing Authority, four by Friends of P-Patch, three by King County, and one by the Seattle School District.

But enough statistics. The best way to convey a sense of how the P-Patch Program works is through stories of particular gardens. The stories offer a few glimpses of how the gardens enhance the environment, build a strong sense of community, promote social equity, and even further international goodwill.

COURTLAND P-PATCH

When Diana Vinh and her family moved to the Courtland Place neighborhood in Rainier Valley in 1997, she didn't want her mother to visit: Vinh knew that her mother would never approve of the neighborhood. Abandoned cars lined the street. Neighboring houses had broken or boarded-up windows. One house, notorious for its twenty-four-hour drug traffic, was known as Crack in the Box. Prostitutes and drug dealers conducted business in the vacant lot at the end of the street. Among Seattle's Police Department officers, Courtland Place was known as the toughest two blocks in Seattle.

After making repeated complaints, Vinh and her neighbors finally got the city to respond with an interdepartmental team in 1998. The Department of Construction and Land Use issued building code violations and the Police Department cracked down on the drug dealing and prostitution. Seattle Public Utilities removed twenty tons of trash. The neighbors got a sense of what their community could be like, but before long the neighborhood had reverted to its previous condition.

Having seen that the remedies offered by the city's best efforts were short-lived, the neighbors decided that they needed to take responsibility for their own community and take matters into their own hands; the best place to start, they decided, would be the vacant lot at the end of the street. They did some research and learned that the lot was an undeveloped street right-of-way. Vinh obtained permission from the Transportation Department to clear the property and build a P-Patch garden.

The garden-building work parties proved to be an effective way to mobilize the community. There was work for people of all ages and abilities: clearing the land; laying irrigation pipe; building fences, gates, a tool shed, compost bins, a picnic area, and twenty-five raised beds; filling the beds with soil and compost; and creating art and signage. The work parties went far to strengthen the neighbors' sense of community and went even farther, driving the illegal activity out of the area more effectively than any police force could.

The Courtland P-Patch was dedicated in June 2000. Now people garden there year-round. In good weather, the community gathers in the P-Patch for barbecues and children's art workshops—and to plan the next project.

> *Project: Courtland Place P-Patch*
> *Sponsor: Courtland Action Team*
> *Location: Spokane Street between 35th and 36th*
> *Avenues South*
> *Year awarded: 1999*
> *Amount awarded: $10,000*
> *Amount leveraged: $12,490*
> *Year completed: 2000*

The Courtland P-Patch catalyzed the redevelopment of the neighborhood, and project has followed project. The first project after the garden was built was to place wheel stops along the street, which would define the edge of the road, and to replace junk cars with street trees. Then the community convinced the Transportation Department to install a sidewalk along the street and lighting in the alley. The community's current project is to build a hill climb in collaboration with an artist from New York. Meanwhile, the neighbors have continued to conduct regular cleanups, and homeowners and landlords alike have continued to upgrade the housing stock. The former Crack in the Box has a new image and a new owner who is active in the community. And Diana's mother is welcome to visit the neighborhood anytime.

A TALE OF TWO HILLSIDES

The predominantly white, middle-income neighborhood of Phinney Ridge and the multiethnic, largely low-income community of North Rainier occupy opposite corners of Seattle. Despite their differences, both have steep hills and both have residents who are passionate about gardening—residents who are so passionate, in fact, that they would move mountains, or at least terrace hillsides, in order to gain garden space. Both communities have creatively turned problem properties into beautiful and productive gardens.

As Northwest 60th Street climbs the hill from Ballard to Phinney Ridge, it stops abruptly at 3rd Avenue Northwest. The upper portion of 60th, although platted as a street, with houses on each side, proved to be too steep to warrant paving. As a result, the right-of-way became an overgrown eyesore. Brambles kept the neighbors on both sides separated from one another. The only use of the undeveloped street was as a home to rats and a raceway for four-wheel-drive vehicles. Neighbors said that the sound of engines being gunned in the late-night competitions to the top was driving them crazy.

I was afraid that the neighbors really were crazy when they applied to the Neighborhood Matching Fund for support to convert this problem property into a community garden. Even someone who never lived in Iowa might have trouble imagining this hillside, with its 30 percent grade, as a garden. But these neighbors imagined it and christened their project Billy Goat's Bluff. With their Matching Fund award, they cleared the brush, dug into the hardpan, and carried 340 hundred-pound timbers and countless tons of goat manure and soil up the hill. The garden rises, terrace by terrace, from 3rd Avenue Northwest nearly all the way to 2nd. At the top, the neighbors created a community gathering place, where I joined the gardeners for a harvest potluck to celebrate the project's completion. I remember the gardeners talking about how the project had brought them together as a community, and I

An undeveloped and overgrown Northwest 60th Street used to separate the neighbors. Photographer unknown.

Now the P-Patch (a.k.a. Billy Goats Bluff) brings the community together. Photograph by Jim Diers.

remember all of us looking down at the lush green gardens and, beyond, across Puget Sound to see a wildly pink-and-gold sunset behind Mount Olympus.

> *Project: Phinney Ridge P-Patch Community Garden*
> *Sponsor: Phinney Ridge Community Council*
> *Location: Northwest 60th Street between 2nd and 3rd*
> *Avenues Northwest*
> *Year awarded: 1989*
> *Amount awarded: $13,500*
> *Amount leveraged: $14,915*
> *Year completed: 1991*

Meanwhile, across town, the residents of the Mt. Baker Village Apartments were building gardens of their own. The apartments are home to Cambodian and Vietnamese refugees with agricultural backgrounds and a desire to grow produce indigenous to their culture. Lacking garden space, they resourcefully terraced a steep hillside between the apartment buildings and Martin Luther King Jr. Way below. They christened it simply Hillside Garden.

There were several problems with the new garden, however. The Mount Baker community was unhappy that the gardeners had used junk to shore up the terraces, creating an eyesore on the hillside that is the gateway to their prestigious neighborhood. The Transportation Department was unhappy because they had not been consulted before the terraces were built, and they worried that the excavation might have destabilized the hillside. Even the gardeners themselves weren't all that happy: the terraced plots, lacking fertile soil and irrigation, were less than ideal.

As a result of all that unhappiness, redevelopment of the Hillside Garden was identified as a high priority in the North Rainier Neighborhood Plan. The community applied to the Neighborhood Matching Fund for help installing a system of concrete panels to better define the terraces and stabilize the hillside. The Matching Fund paid for the materials, and the labor—all of it—was donated by the community, mostly by residents of Mt. Baker Village. Volunteers used picks and shovels to sculpt terraces out of the dense, clay-filled soil. To make the retaining wall, they

Community members of all generations work together to build the Hillside Garden in Mount Baker. Photograph by Wendy Hughes-Jelen; reprinted with permission.

hauled tons of concrete panels and rocks down the steep slope. As many as sixty volunteers of all ages turned out for work parties every weekend for two summers.

I was helping one Saturday when I saw an elderly woman with a walker come with very small, slow steps out of Mt. Baker Village across the parking lot to the top of the garden. She eased herself onto a large pile of rocks and began to put rocks into a bucket. When she was finished with that one, she began to fill another. A young teenager picked up each full bucket and passed the rocks to the next person in the intergenerational bucket brigade that traversed the hillside. The full buckets went down and the empty buckets went back up the hillside all day long.

At one point while we were working, a car stopped on the street below and the driver opened her window and shouted, "Can I help?" There was no hesitation to welcome her. In the course of the afternoon, she mentioned that she lived a couple of miles away and had been on her way to work out at the health club. She enjoyed volunteering on the project so much that she returned on subsequent weekends and got such a good workout that she dropped her health club membership.

With the concrete panels fully installed now, the terraces are more secure and look much tidier. Deep compost and an irrigation system make the gardens much more productive. The residents of Mt. Baker Village are justly proud of what they have accomplished, and they cherish the many new friendships that grew within their community and with the surrounding neighborhood.

> *Project: The Hillside Garden*
> *Sponsor: Mt. Baker Housing Association*
> *Location: Martin Luther King Jr. Way South and South McClellan Street*
> *Years awarded: 2000 and 2001*
> *Amount awarded: $46,400*
> *Amount leveraged: $54,063*
> *Year completed: 2002*

BELLTOWN P-PATCH: A SAGA

In between Seattle's downtown and uptown is Belltown, Seattle's densest neighborhood. With its many apartment buildings and new condominium towers, and more continually on the rise, no one could doubt that Belltown needed more green space than its one tiny park provided. Community members lobbied city officials to purchase Belltown's last remaining vacant lot for a P-Patch that would double as a garden and a park. They were persistent and creative, several chalking their petitions on the sidewalks outside city hall and one dressing in a bee costume to testify at city council hearings. Finally in 1993, the city purchased the one-eighth block to preserve as open space. From its past as the site of homeless encampments, the overgrown lot was littered with trash, including needles and broken glass. The city had no money to develop the garden, so the community turned to the Neighborhood Matching Fund for support.

In 1992, Belltown P-Patch was just a hope and a sign. Photograph by Catherine Anstett.

Today the P-Patch is the site of public art, renovated cottages, bountiful gardens, and a vibrant community. Photograph by Jim Diers.

Matching Fund money paid for what couldn't be donated, and the community's volunteer labor and its donated goods and services took care of the rest. Projects created by a community reflect that community's character, and the Belltown P-Patch reflects the creativity of Belltown's artists. The concrete retaining wall on the garden's west side is covered with large mosaic murals of birds, bees, and flowers. An artistic steel fence surrounding the garden depicts various vegetables. Handmade garden tools and small sculptures of flora and fauna have been welded into the garden's steel gates. Just past the gates is a solar-powered fountain. The individual garden plots are bordered by rocks, and each plot contains additional artwork that reflects each gardener's tastes and talents as much as the flowers and vegetables that get planted. The Belltown P-Patch is an urban oasis for many more people than those who actually do the gardening there.

Project: Belltown P-Patch
Sponsor: Friends of Belltown P-Patch
Location: Elliott Avenue and Vine Street
Year awarded: 1993
Amount awarded: $47,876
Amount leveraged: $50,825
Year completed: 1995

The garden's dedication was to be preceded by a parade winding through the neighborhood to the garden. I accepted the invitation to join the marchers, but I was a little late arriving at the local costume shop where everyone was told to meet. Unfortunately, they had run out of costumes—or perhaps fortunately, since almost everyone was dressed in drag. So, wearing the business suit I had worn to the office that morning and feeling like one of the oddest characters on the scene, I joined the others to parade up and down the streets of Belltown and through its quirky shops and taverns. By the time we reached the garden, more than four hundred people had turned out to celebrate the dedication.

In 1998, the Belltown community had to lobby the city again. The owner of the property to the south of the P-Patch had plans to develop a large office building that would have kept the entire garden in shade most of the day. The city finally responded to community pressure by purchasing the very expensive property for park space. Part of the city's plan was to demolish the three dilapidated cottages on the site. The community, however, had something else in mind. The community argued to preserve the historic cottages, which had been built for cannery workers in 1917 and which now provided a scale refreshingly unlike anything else in this neighborhood of tall buildings. When the Parks Department protested that it lacked the money to renovate and maintain the cottages, the community announced that it would renovate the cottages themselves with materials purchased through the Neighborhood Matching Fund. Today, the beautifully restored cottages are leased by a writers-in-residence program: the writers enrich the community's cultural experience and keep an eye on the P-Patch, which had previously experienced some problems with vandalism.

> Project: Belltown Cottages
> Sponsor: Friends of Belltown P-Patch
> Location: 2512 to 2516 Elliott Avenue
> Year awarded: 2001
> Amount awarded: $200,000
> Amount leveraged: $253,401
> Year completed: 2003

Belltown P-Patch has also been the catalyst for an even more ambitious community project called Growing Vine Street. As part of Belltown's neighborhood planning process, the community envisioned expanding the green of the P-Patch into adjacent Vine Street and up the hill for eight blocks: a winding, narrow street that would be lined with art, trees, plants, ponds, and a creek.

The first part of that project to appear was 81 Vine Street, a 1914 building renovated by Carolyn Geise for her architectural offices. When Geise added a fourth floor for live-work lofts, she built in a system that captures rainwater and routes it to a roof garden. The rainwater runs through

On Vine Street, no opportunity for gardening is overlooked. Photograph by Jim Diers.

an artfully designed trough filled with plants. The water sustains the plants and the plants serve to filter the water, which then flows down a unique downspout with offshoot planters in which ornamental grasses grow. A second downspout leads to one of five gigantic fingers extending from a ten-foot-tall blue cylinder. The *Beckoning Cistern*, created by local artist Buster Simpson, stores what Geise refers to as the "headwaters of Vine Creek." Several new buildings along Vine Street are currently being designed to serve as tributaries to Vine Creek.

> *Project: Cistern Steps*
> *Sponsor: Growing Vine Street*
> *Location: Vine Street and Western Avenue*
> *Years awarded: 1998 and 2002*
> *Amount awarded: $121,572*
> *Amount leveraged: $178,870*
> *Year completed: 2003*

The Beckoning Cistern holds the water for Vine Creek. Photograph by Jim Diers.

In the grand plan for Vine Street, the run-off will be collected in a series of cisterns, from which it will flow through a runnel to cascade down a flight of steps. Plants in intermittent retention ponds will further filter pollutants from the water. The first section of this ingenious system, currently under construction, will irrigate the P-Patch.

CASCADE RAIN HARVEST

Growing Vine Street, innovative as it is, builds on the pioneering work of Cascade, a neighborhood just north of downtown. In 1996, the Cascade community conducted a series of workshops and subsequently produced a handbook and design guidelines for sustainable urban water flow. Eager to put those guidelines into practice, the community worked with a University of Washington class to design and build two projects that they call Rain Harvest.

In the first project, along the Republican Street hillside above Yale Avenue, a downspout carries roof run-off down the side of a commercial building and into a second-story window for use by a glass studio. Most of the water, though, continues down to street level, where it enters a cistern adjacent to the sidewalk. Gravity carries water from the cistern through a hose to holding tanks that release the water into a series of planter boxes that run the length of the sidewalk.

The Cascade P-Patch is the site of the second Rain Harvest project. Rainwater from the roof of the next-door community center flows into four dozen fifty-five-gallon barrels and an underground cistern with a capacity of five thousand gallons. Faucets labeled Captured Water supply 40 percent of the water used by the P-Patch; water from the cistern also irrigates a nursery for plants salvaged from construction sites, and it will soon flush the toilets in the community center. With the cistern covered by a large gazebo and the rain barrels surrounded by an attractive trellis, the system is an aesthetic asset as well as an environmental asset.

INTERBAY COMPOST

In a way that is more eventful than most, the Interbay P-Patch is the center of the community for the 167 households who have plots there. The gardeners, who come from many walks of life—teachers, lawyers, computer technicians, homeless people, retirees, an actress—gather here to socialize, to recreate, and to engage in community service together, donating about two tons of produce to food banks each year. They share Friday dinners and Saturday lunches in the central plaza. They even eat Christmas dinner together and exchange gifts. The larger community is always welcome to visit, and sometimes they are especially invited for a salmon barbecue, an oyster feed, or a baroque concert. Interbay also hosts classes on organic gardening and composting. At least two couples have been married there, and one long-time gardener had his ashes scattered on the site after a memorial service held at the garden.

Adversity has a way of pulling people together and Interbay gardeners, from the start, have had their share of adversity. The one-acre garden was created in 1974 on the site of a thirty-acre former landfill: extensive work was needed to create fertile soil where there had been only garbage capped by heavy clay. Several years later when a golf course was developed next door, the gardeners had to fight to keep the garden from being swallowed by it. They succeeded that time but in 1991 were unable to stop the construction of a driving range that forced them to move the garden several hundred yards. The gardeners had to move again in 1997 when the driving range was reoriented to reduce the glare of the sun for the golfers. Moving a garden—infrastructure, soil, plants, and all—is never easy, but with each move the garden just got better. The gardeners' relationship with their neighbors got better too when the golf course sponsored a P-Patch Open as a fund-raiser for the garden and made a golf cart available for work parties.

Because the garden started with a dump and because of the gardeners' experience with turning adversity into opportunity, composting is less a practice than a way of life at Interbay. Every Saturday at compost socials, the gardeners make compost together. There are test plots where the gardeners experiment with different mixtures of compost. They chop up all of the garden's dead plants, then mix in leaves from neighboring yards and parks, and then they get creative. One gardener brings regular supplies of coffee grounds from his job at Starbucks. Jon Rowley, a gardener with connections to the seafood industry, heard about sixty thousand pounds of oysters that were going to be dumped because they had reached their expiration date; he had them delivered to Interbay instead, where they were turned into compost.

Rowley and Kate McDermott met at a compost social, so it seemed only appropriate to hold their wedding ceremony at Interbay. In lieu of traditional wedding gifts, they asked all their guests to bring something for the compost pile, which McDermott and Rowley would turn as part of the wedding. Wedding compost ingredients came from all over,

I compost my termination letter at the Interbay P-Patch. Photograph by Bradley Enghaus, Pacific Publishing; reprinted with permission.

among them a banana peel from Julia Child, buffalo droppings, and even a tax refund check.

Six weeks later, on September 11, 2001, terrorists attacked the World Trade Center and the Pentagon. In Seattle, seventy-five thousand people expressed their grief and showed their solidarity with the victims and their families by bringing bouquets of flowers as a makeshift memorial at Seattle Center's International Fountain. Approximately a million flowers encircled the fountain by the end of the four-day vigil.

It would have seemed almost sacrilegious to haul the decaying flowers to the dump, so the Interbay gardeners volunteered to compost them. With other volunteers, they separated the flowers from the rest: written messages, children's drawings, stuffed animals, flags, candle stubs, prayer beads, and other memorial gifts, along with any plastic and wire attached to the flowers.

Eighty gardeners turned out at Interbay the next Saturday to create the memorial compost. They came with leaves and other "browns" to mix with the eighty cubic yards of flowers from the vigil. They spent all day hauling, chopping, and mixing. When they were done, Rowley declared, "The now-steaming piles are, and will always be, symbols and agents for hope and renewal."

The finished compost served as the basis for a memorial garden that was dedicated at Seattle Center one year later. Those attending the ceremony each received a scoop of compost along with a tulip bulb. The final yard of memorial compost was delivered to Manhattan by a delegation of Interbay gardeners accompanied by city councilmember Richard Conlin. They presented it at the rededication of Liberty Community Gardens, which had been destroyed when it was used as an emergency staging area for the rescue workers.

When I was not reappointed by Mayor-Elect Greg Nickels in 2002, the gardeners decided that Interbay should be the site of my own renewal. They invited me to join the roster of celebrity composters. I felt deeply honored. Previous celebrities included famous chefs, elected officials, and the first bicyclist to ride naked in the Fremont Solstice Parade. The celebrities' names are inscribed on the bins of the compost that they turned. A good crowd turned out for my induction. I brought along photocopies of my termination letter and asked people to shred them as I read it aloud. Then, as I turned the compost, people took turns adding the shredded letters. I told the crowd that Interbay had taught me an important lesson: "When the world gives you lemons, make lemonade, and when someone gives you shit, make compost."

BRADNER GARDENS PARK

No matter that the famous site in Berkeley had the name first, I always think of Bradner Gardens as the real people's park. The community fought for the land and then took the lead in planning and building the park. Today community members use and maintain it—and continue to build. No question: the park belongs to the people.

In 1995, it had looked as though the community might lose the land. Although the Parks Department owned the acre and a half, city officials had decided that the best use of the land was for market-rate housing. Located on the ridge above the Interstate 90 tunnel, the property has commanding views of downtown and the Olympic Mountains beyond.

With little other open space to call its own, the community rallied to keep the park land as a park. The neighbors already had a small P-Patch on the property and had used the Neighborhood Matching Fund to develop a plan for the remainder of the site: they had a considerable investment in the land. City officials weren't sympathetic, however. So the neighbors launched an initiative campaign to enact a law making it illegal to use Parks Department–owned land for non-park purposes. When they obtained enough signatures to place the initiative on the ballot, city councilmembers saw the writing on the wall and enacted the law themselves in 1997. The property had been saved for the community to enjoy as a park.

As a park, however, the property still had a long way to go. Its past as the site of a school was still evident in several rundown portables in a sea of cracked asphalt. The group turned to the Neighborhood Matching Fund for help in implementing their plan.

After forty thousand hours of volunteer labor, accumulated through weekly work parties over six years, Bradner Gardens Park is now a reality. The first thing you see, as you enter the park through a trellis made of iron and stone, is a large pavilion with a leaf-shaped roof, which, along with other architectural elements, was contributed by the Design-Build Program at the University of Washington School of Architecture. The pavilion is surrounded by all kinds of gardens. Of the sixty-one P-Patch plots, fifteen are gardened by members of the Mien tribe from Laos. Housing for persons with disabilities is located below the park, so there are wheelchair-accessible gardens. Near the Lighthouse for the Blind, the park contains tactile and sensory gardens for visitors who are visually impaired. The community's many children have their own garden. The park even includes a wildlife habitat. Seattle Tree Stewards sponsor a garden featuring twenty varieties of street trees to help people choose what to plant on their parking strips and, of course, to inspire them to plant street trees in the first place. Native plants, drought-tolerant plants, and other demonstration gardens are maintained by Seattle Tilth and King County Master Gardeners. The diverse vegetation aptly reflects the diversity of the surrounding neighborhood.

This bench, which depicts the life cycle of the salmon, is one of many artworks that seem to sprout out of Bradner Gardens Park. Photograph by Jim Diers.

Project: Bradner Gardens Park
Sponsor: Friends of Bradner Gardens Park
Location: South Grand Street and 29th Avenue South
Years awarded: 1995, 1997, 1998, and 1999
Amount awarded: $209,500
Amount leveraged: $1,100,000
Year completed: 2003

There is much more to the park than its gardens, however. A new basketball court is in constant use. Its backboards are easily adjustable for use by players of any size. The playground has an agricultural theme and features a full-scale sculpture of a tractor pulling an enormous tree stump out of the ground.

Art is everywhere. A neighborhood artist carved a bench showing the life cycle of the salmon. Students at Coyote Junior High created a ceramic vine on top of the short wall that runs the length of the basketball court;

Seeing a working windmill in the center of Seattle warms my Iowan heart. Photograph by Ian Edelstein, City of Seattle; reprinted with permission.

the vine eventually climbs into outer space. A metal fence incorporates dozens of garden tools welded into its design. Funky and distinctively handcrafted scarecrows guard the plots. Even the hose bibs are works of folk art.

One of the park's most distinctive elements is its unique water feature. Run-off drains into a pond at the low end of the property and, although the pond added character to the park, the stagnant water attracted mosquitoes. The gardeners responded by purchasing a windmill. (How does one purchase a windmill? On the Internet, of course.) The Depression-era windmill from a farm in Iowa was shipped in pieces and reassembled at Bradner Gardens. The windmill pumps the pond water to the opposite end of the park, where it becomes a stream that runs over and around boulders, under a bridge, and back into the pond. The mosquito problem was solved, and the practice of recycling was raised to new heights.

Likewise, an old storage shed and a restroom were recycled to become an environmentally friendly community center. Solar panels not only provide all of the energy needed by the center, but they generate excess electricity for use by Seattle City Light. The walls in the meeting room are covered with panels made from pressed sunflower seeds. Beautiful tile mosaics with a garden theme now adorn the formerly graffiti-covered walls of the restroom.

Bradner Gardens has fostered a tremendous sense of community. Neighbors still come out for regular work parties, and they also come together for everything from barbecues to poetry readings. Testimony to that newfound community spirit came in a letter I received from a family that lived across the street from the park. The letter was written on motel stationery: "Last week, when our precious home burned down, so many neighbors from the Bradner Park and Gardens project took the time, energy, and kindness to comfort our family. . . . If there is ever anything we can do to keep the chain of kindness linking neighbor to neighbor, please let us know. We left our home with nothing, but we are spirit-rich."

CULTIVATING FRIENDSHIPS WITH HAVANA

When Seattle observed the twenty-fifth anniversary of its P-Patch Program in 1998, we invited Eugenio Fuster Chepe to help us celebrate. Chepe is director of Havana's Department of Urban Agriculture. I couldn't wait to brag about Seattle's fifty community gardens. Fortunately, before I had a chance to embarrass myself, Chepe was talking about the 1,700 community gardens he manages in Havana. He also told me about the million trees that his department had helped people in Havana to plant.

All of that had been accomplished since 1992 when Havana faced severe food shortages due to the breakup of the Soviet Union and the ongoing U.S. embargo. A lack of refrigerated trucks meant that fresh produce could not be shipped from the countryside without much of it spoiling in transit. The solution was to convert Havana's vacant lots into hundreds of community gardens. All of Havana's community gardens are organic because of both a strong environmental ethic and a lack of commercial fertilizers and pesticides. Similarly, trees were planted both to help clean the air and to provide fruit and nuts for eating and to provide organic matter for composting.

With our shared interests in organic gardening, urban reforestation, and community building, we realized that we had much to learn from one another and agreed to enter into a sister department relationship. Chepe invited me to come to Havana to see his programs firsthand and to discuss ways in which our departments could work together.

As I drove into Havana from the airport in March 1999, I was struck by the great number of community gardens that lined the road, most accompanied by produce stands. I toured a dozen gardens during my stay and talked with the proud gardeners. The members of a cooperative of revolutionary war veterans bicycle to the countryside each day to grow food for the senior centers and child-care centers in their neighborhood. In the low-income neighborhood of La Guinera, young people have organized themselves as the Friends of Nature to undertake a variety of environmental projects, including a community garden.

I was especially impressed with the way in which gardens were integrated with schools. A large garden I visited was surrounded by an elementary school, a middle school, a school for the deaf, and a school for swimmers. The students work in the garden for two hours each day to fulfill their community service requirement. Culinary arts classes teach students how to prepare meals from the fresh produce that is then served in the school cafeterias. I may never have eaten better tasting tomatoes, certainly not in my school cafeteria.

Chepe's department has developed sophisticated biological controls for pests and disease, and they are for sale at municipally owned garden stores. Seeds and tools can be purchased as well. Advice on growing and composting is dispensed for free by the extension agents. The store I visited was actively promoting the use of worm bins, a technology that Chepe had brought back with him from Seattle. A poster hanging over the bins showed worms with revolutionary caps crawling through the soil, with the caption "The revolution is underground."

Before I returned home, Chepe suggested that the gardeners of Havana and Seattle plant trees dedicated to one another on Earth Day 2000. Joyce Moty, who led the effort to build Bradner Gardens, subsequently volunteered to plant a tree in honor of the people of Havana. When two leaders of the La Guinera neighborhood visited Seattle, I took them to Bradner and showed them where we intended to plant the tree. Moty announced that she would sew a Cuban flag and fly it together with the United States flag from the park's old flagpole. The Havana delegates were moved to tears.

Steve Badanes, creator of *Fremont Troll*, was at Bradner Gardens at the same time, working with his students from the University of Washington's Design-Build Program. When I introduced Badanes to our Havana guests, he immediately declared that the program's next project would be in Cuba. I put him in touch with Chepe, who invited Badanes to bring his class to Havana to design and build a gathering hall for community gardeners.

A delegation of forty-five students and artists flew to Havana in February 2001. They spent three weeks working alongside Havana gardeners to convert an old 30-by-150-foot chicken coop into what is now known as the Chief Seattle Social Club. The delegation, believed to be the first officially sanctioned builders from the United States to work in modern Cuba, also installed a foil ceiling to cool the building. To provide sufficient headroom, they excavated two feet of soil before installing a terrazzo floor. Broken concrete from the old floor was recycled to create a sidewalk around the building. Between the sidewalk and the building, students, artists, and gardeners created a drainage swale with beautiful landscaping. A brick patio leads to an entrance comprising glass mosaics, decorative ironwork, and a plaque commemorating the organizations that worked together in "cultivating friendships."

6

SUSTAINING COMMUNITIES

The Neighborhood Planning Program

As a former community organizer, I hated neighborhood planning. Planning was too often the city's substitute for action. Plans came out of city hall with only token involvement of the community. Not surprisingly, the planners were the only ones who really understood or cared about the plans' vision and recommendations. With no constituency to implement them, the plans usually just sat on the shelf.

So when I was appointed director of the new Office of Neighborhoods, although I was expected to hire planners, I hired organizers instead. I wanted to make sure that all communities had a strong voice and could utilize the city's programs and services. It seemed to me that marginalized communities in particular would benefit more from organizers than from planners.

Yet planning was clearly called for by the Neighborhood Planning and Assistance Program that my office was charged with administering. With no planners on staff, I had to figure out how to do the planning. I turned to the only resource available, the Neighborhood Matching Fund. With the support of the City Neighborhood Council, we made planning an eligible use of the Matching Fund. The result was a very different, bottom-up approach to neighborhood planning. That model of planning differs from traditional planning in five major respects.

First, with the new model, the community rather than city government initiates the planning process. When the city initiated plans, often the community was either uninterested or suspicious about the city's real motives: "What are they going to try to get past the community this time?" The community won't initiate a plan through the Neighborhood Matching Fund unless it is clear about exactly why a plan is needed. After all, planning is a lot of work and, if planning is not really needed, that energy could be better expended elsewhere.

Second, the new model lets the community define its own planning area. When the city developed plans, it often used census tracts to determine boundaries. The community instead defines the neighborhood by its own understanding of the neighborhood, usually in accordance with the boundaries identified in community council bylaws.

Third, the community identifies its own scope of work. City plans tended to focus on the function of the department that was doing the planning, typically land use or community development. When the community is in charge, community members plan for what is important to them, whether that is economic development, public safety, human services, recreation, open space, transportation, affordable housing, education, history, or arts and culture. Often, communities want to address all these elements with a comprehensive plan: communities tend to think more holistically than do city departments.

Fourth, the community can hire its own planner rather than end up with whatever planner the city assigns. They can look for a planner who works well with people in addition to having good technical skills. Having the planner be accountable to the community makes an inestimable difference in the planning process.

Finally, with the new model, community members become much more involved in the planning process because they are required to come up with the match. Since it might prove difficult to conduct successful fund-raisers for planners' salaries, the community's match usually consists of hundreds of volunteers. Community volunteers are active in every step of the process: submitting the application, hiring the planner, drafting and conducting surveys, and developing the vision and recommendations. That means that people understand the plan and feel ownership of it. They hold the city accountable for implementing the plan and, moreover, they take responsibility for much of the implementation themselves.

Coincidentally, the first community that chose to develop a plan through the Neighborhood Matching Fund was Southeast Seattle, where

I had worked as an organizer. Through discussions in their district council, all twelve community councils and business associations in this racially and economically diverse community decided to develop a joint plan. They formed a planning committee comprising one representative from each organization, and they selected SouthEast Effective Development (SEED), a local community development corporation, to serve as their consultant.

Although many plans for Southeast Seattle had been developed over the years, this would be the most inclusive planning effort to date. The planning committee members made sure that their respective stakeholder groups stayed well informed and actively engaged throughout the process. As part of the effort to broaden participation, the planning committee employed an innovative outreach strategy. Survey forms were distributed in the most racially diverse places in the community, namely, the schools. To increase the rate of return, the committee persuaded the local Darigold plant to promise a free ice cream cone for every survey completed. This outreach strategy cost little but netted nearly 1,500 completed surveys.

Not surprisingly, the resulting Southeast Seattle Action Plan had broad community support. When the plan was presented to city council in 1991, council chambers was packed with community representatives demanding that the plan be adopted—be adopted *and* implemented. The city agreed to prepare an annual progress report, and the mayor himself delivered it each year at a large community meeting.

The city followed through on all of the key plan recommendations. The small, deteriorating Rainier Community Center was demolished and replaced with the largest community center in Seattle. Millions of dollars were spent to repave the community's major arterials. Additional street and alley lighting was installed to enhance public safety. Priority went to the processing of permits in target areas along Rainier Avenue South, facilitating major new commercial development. The city purchased a vacant block near Rainier Avenue South and South Dearborn Street for intensive residential development, including co-housing and homes for first-time buyers.

Equally important, the community did its part to implement the plan.

Much of the residential and commercial development was undertaken by SEED and other community-based organizations. Local businesses partnered with the city to improve the facades of their storefronts and the appearance of adjacent streets and sidewalks. With help from the Neighborhood Matching Fund, the community built playgrounds, painted murals, and planted street trees as recommended in the plan. The Southeast Seattle Action Plan is one important reason that more Matching Fund projects have been completed in Southeast Seattle than in any other part of the city.

Other neighborhoods soon followed Southeast Seattle's example. Queen Anne, the International District, Pike-Pine, Roosevelt, and North Beacon Hill developed their own comprehensive plans. Some communities initiated issue-specific plans targeting parking, traffic, public safety, historic resources, or business district revitalization. Other groups used the Neighborhood Matching Fund to create site-specific plans for new parks or playgrounds. By 1994, planning had become popular with neighborhood activists—but that was about to change.

PLANNING FOR GROWTH

Community leaders, including some neighborhood activists, had successfully lobbied the Washington state legislature to enact the Growth Management Act in 1990. They feared that the natural environment that was attracting people to Puget Sound was being jeopardized by sprawl as people took residence in the foothills and on former farmlands and wetlands. The enacted legislation mandated that King County draw a growth boundary to protect its rural areas and assign growth targets to its urban centers. The City of Seattle, in turn, was required to develop a plan for adding 50,000 to 60,000 households and 140,000 jobs by 2014.

The resulting Comprehensive Plan, approved in 1994, seemed to me to be quite neighborhood friendly. The plan, "Towards a Sustainable Seattle," was based on the values of environmental stewardship, social equity, economic opportunity, and community. It protected single-family neighborhoods and called for concentrating growth around neighborhood business districts—a good transportation and economic development strategy. The plan included provisions for adding open space and other amenities as neighborhoods became more dense.

Seattle's Comprehensive Plan, however, was not well received by many neighborhood activists. It had been written by planners with excellent technical skills but less expertise at working with the community. The plan established growth targets for "urban villages" defined by boundaries that few people recognized. Many Seattleites saw these urban villages as a threat to their beloved neighborhoods. Few people read the entire plan—for the very good reason that it was more than six hundred pages long. Consequently, the plan made great fodder for demagogues who were happy to summarize it with their own spin. Opposition to the plan grew behind the banner of a Neighborhood Rights Campaign.

Elected officials were quick to point out that the Comprehensive Plan only provided the framework for further, more detailed planning. Because neighborhoods are so important to Seattle's citizens and because each neighborhood has its own character, the officials said, the next stage of planning would occur at the neighborhood level. Mayor Rice asked me to involve neighborhood leaders in developing a proposal for how that neighborhood planning should be carried out. Fortunately, I had the assistance of Karma Ruder, the director of our Neighborhood Service Centers.

Ruder and I invited neighborhood leaders to a meeting at the University of Washington to plan how to plan. The topic seemed dry at best. I didn't expect much of a turnout on a sunny Saturday in May, but 250 people came and spent the entire day in animated discussion. The upshot was that they liked the basic Neighborhood Matching Fund model, in which the community initiates the plan, defines its own boundaries and scope of work, hires its own planner, and is integrally involved throughout the process.

However, the participants also identified a couple of shortcomings with the Matching Fund model of planning. One concern was that most of the plans were sponsored by only one organization, and there is no one organization in any neighborhood that adequately represents all of the stakeholders. As a result, there had been times when opposition to a plan surfaced only after community members had spent considerable time developing it.

A second concern with the model was that it was too independent of city government. Participants in the Saturday meeting emphasized that a community needs advice and support prior to hiring its planners; the planning process could benefit from the information and expertise of city departments, and successful plan implementation would require ownership by city departments as well as by the community. In short, people wanted a more collaborative model. Meeting participants selected eleven representatives (a.k.a. The Gang of Eleven) to work with Ruder and me to develop that model.

The resultant program, as supported by Mayor Rice and the Seattle City Council, included a pot of $4.5 million from which neighborhoods could hire their own planning experts. Thirty-seven communities, encompassing 66 percent of Seattle's population and 56 percent of its land, were eligible to participate. These eligible communities, as defined by the Comprehensive Plan, included one "distressed" neighborhood, two industrial areas, and thirty-four "urban centers" and "urban villages." The urban centers and urban villages are neighborhoods where the greatest growth is expected to occur because the area's preexisting infrastructure and zoning can accommodate it. Neighborhood planning was intended to involve the affected communities in determining how to encourage growth while enhancing the communities' quality of life.

To facilitate the collaborative planning process called for by the community, Mayor Rice established the Neighborhood Planning Office in 1995 and appointed Ruder to be its director. Ruder hired ten project managers, each of whom was assigned to three or four of the potential planning areas. The project managers' job was to inform the community in those planning areas about the opportunity to plan as well as the city's expectations; help the community in each area organize a planning committee and contract for consultant services; provide the community with ongoing guidance, support, and troubleshooting; ensure that the community complied with city requirements; ensure that the relevant city departments were actively engaged throughout the planning and review process; and serve as a link between the various planning efforts.

All thirty-seven communities were told that it was their choice whether or not to initiate a plan. If they decided not to, the city would defer to the Comprehensive Plan. Communities that chose to plan needed to use the Comprehensive Plan, including its growth targets, as their point of reference. Communities could use the planning process to propose amendments to the Comprehensive Plan but would need to present a convincing case to the city council, which, as the final authority on all plans, would then vote on whether to adopt each plan.

Interested communities were asked to take two initial steps. One step was to define its planning area. The community was encouraged to utilize the existing boundaries of one or more neighborhoods, although the planning area had to encompass the urban village as defined in the Comprehensive Plan.

The second step was to organize a planning committee that was genuinely representative of the planning area's major stakeholders. The planning committee had to represent more than just the area's community council and business association. The Neighborhood Planning Office developed and analyzed demographic profiles of the neighborhoods to ensure that the makeup of each committee accurately reflected the community's makeup, including people of color, property owners, and tenants. Any major institution, such as a hospital or university, in a neighborhood needed to be represented as well.

Once a representative planning committee had been established and the planning area had been identified, the community was eligible to apply for $10,000 to undertake the first phase of its planning process. In that initial phase, the planning committee conducted surveys and public meetings to define a vision and a scope of work that addressed the community's primary interests and concerns.

The planning committee was also accountable for developing a detailed outreach plan. The city's expectation was that all community members would be kept informed and that as many as possible would be actively involved throughout the planning process. To ensure that recent immigrants, persons with disabilities, youth, and other marginalized populations participated in the process, each planning committee was given an "outreach tool kit" to help identify media and organizations serving those populations, resources for translation and interpretation, and ideas for effective outreach techniques.

When a scope of work and outreach plan had been developed to the satisfaction of the project manager, the planning committee was eligible to apply for money for the second phase. A planning group could receive $60,000 to $100,000 depending on the planning area's size and complexity. As in the first phase, the money could be used for consultants and for expenses related to outreach.

This second phase was the actual planning. Each planning committee organized subcommittees to focus on specific issues or areas of interest, such as transportation, open space, housing, human services, public safety, and business district revitalization. The subcommittees worked with consultants to prepare background reports and develop a range of optional strategies to address the issues the subcommittees had identified.

Those options were presented through display boards and brief presentations at an Alternatives Fair to which the entire community was invited. The feedback and additional ideas generated at this event informed the work of the subcommittees. The fair also provided a prime opportunity to recruit more people to participate.

Following the fair, the subcommittees and their consultants conducted further studies and additional outreach. They discussed their findings at length in an effort to develop recommendations that would fulfill their plan's goals and that would be supported by the community. To verify that support, the draft recommendations were mailed to all households, businesses, and property owners in the planning area. The mailing included an invitation to vote on the recommendations either by mail or by attending a validation event.

Recommendations were revised based on the vote, and the final plan was submitted to the Mayor's Strategic Planning Office. Although various city departments had been advising the community throughout the planning process, this was the executive's opportunity to advise the city council. The Strategic Planning Office drafted policy language for the Comprehensive Plan and ordinances for zoning changes, based on the recommendations of the neighborhood plan, to the extent that city departments were in agreement. It also prepared a matrix that delineated city responses and commitments needed to implement each recommendation, together with the estimated costs for the city and expected roles for the community.

With the dedicated leadership of Richard Conlin, the Neighborhoods Committee of the city council then reviewed each neighborhood plan and the executive's response. The Neighborhoods Committee held a public hearing at a neighborhood site to determine the extent to which the plan had the community's support. In most cases, the planning committee, the larger community, and the executive were in agreement, but sometimes the Neighborhoods Committee had to mediate differences or choose sides. The city council finally adopted policy language and related legislation, approved the matrices, and formally approved all of the plans in 1998 and 1999. Each neighborhood plan had taken two to four years to produce.

The Neighborhood Planning Program was remarkable in many ways. Given the original controversy, it was amazing that all thirty-seven eligible neighborhoods decided to participate. Even more astonishing was the fact that, despite the truly daunting amount of work required, all the plans were completed and approved.

It seems notable that no plan recommended zoning changes that would reduce a neighborhood's development capacity. A couple of plans stipulated even higher growth targets than were established by the Comprehensive Plan. All thirty-seven plans included strategies for accommodating growth.

The community's remarkable buy-in to the Comprehensive Plan can be attributed to the way in which the community was empowered to develop its own strategies tailored to the unique character of each neighborhood; as it turned out, the neighborhoods were less concerned about growth than with how growth would be achieved. Some plans called for legalizing accessory dwelling units and cottage housing in their neighborhoods, a strategy that other neighborhoods had opposed when local officials had earlier tried to impose it citywide. Some of the neighborhoods that objected to accessory dwelling units opted for more multifamily housing, and their plans included design guidelines to help developers work effectively with the community. Wallingford worked with developers to design a grand public stairway between two new apartment buildings to connect the neighborhood with Gas Works Park below. The Ballard plan calls for replacing a vacant supermarket and its surrounding parking lot in the heart of their neighborhood with a civic center that will include a 1.6-acre park, a new library, and a new Neighborhood Service Center intended to attract new multifamily housing around the perimeter. Neighborhoods on proposed transit lines planned for station-oriented development. In the University District, the neighborhood plan calls for replacing large-surface parking lots with mixed-use buildings and underground parking. The Pike-Pine plan, on the other hand, recommends a reduction in parking requirements because the neighborhood is near downtown and is well served by public transportation—a strategy for making housing more affordable. Again and again, the neighborhood plans demonstrated that communities, when given responsibility, act responsibly.

The Neighborhood Planning Program also demonstrated that people, when they are genuinely empowered, get involved. About thirty thousand people participated in the program, thanks to committed neighborhood leaders and their creative outreach strategies. The planners tried to engage the community on its own turf whether that took them into a school classroom, a senior center, a religious institution, or, as with the Uptown planners, behind a card table on a busy street corner. They made public meetings fun by disguising them as celebrations and multicultural festivals complete with food and entertainment.

The unprecedented level of participation meant that the community expected much more out of these neighborhood plans than they had out of previous plans. As Mayor Rice put it, "We have let the genie out of the bottle and we'll never get it back in." At that point, it was up to the city to deliver.

IMPLEMENTING NEIGHBORHOOD PLANS

The thirty-seven neighborhood plans were nearing completion when Paul Schell took office as mayor in 1998. Despite high community expectations for action on 4,277 plan recommendations, no dedicated resources had been budgeted except a one-time Early Implementation Fund of $1,850,000 ($50,000 per plan). Mayor Schell may have been tempted to disclaim any responsibility for the Neighborhood Planning Program, but instead he made plan implementation his top priority. The mayor charged the Department of Neighborhoods with managing plan implementation, and he moved the Neighborhood Planning Office into the department to facilitate a smooth transition from planning to implementation. Working closely with councilmember Conlin, Mayor Schell devised a three-part strategy to implement neighborhood plans.

The first part took advantage of the fact that, although the city was already spending most of its regular budget in the neighborhoods, the money was not necessarily being spent on the communities' priorities. The challenge was to move from business-as-usual to implementing the neighborhood plans. The mayor realized that this sea change would be impossible unless city government decentralized, enabling departments to focus on each of the thirty-seven plans and to work together with each other and with the community. Coordination would be essential because so many of the recommendations required the participation of multiple departments.

Some departments had already decentralized, but no two departments were decentralized with the same boundaries. The mayor consulted with department heads and decided to organize Seattle into six sectors, with the Ship Canal, Interstate 90, and Interstate 5 as dividing lines. In addition to being highly visible, those boundaries correspond to Seattle Police Department precincts, and most of the thirteen neighborhood districts fit neatly within them. The mayor directed departments to move toward decentralizing their operations into the six sectors and, in the interim, to assign to each sector a manager who was empowered to speak for the department.

At the mayor's direction, the Department of Neighborhoods hired a manager for each of the six sectors, to coordinate an interdepartmental team and to work with all of the plan stewardship groups in their sector. The stewardship groups are successors to the planning committees; they are community-based groups that were designated in each plan to advocate and assist with implementation. They play a crucial role by holding the city accountable, clarifying and prioritizing plan recommendations, mobilizing community resources, and keeping the community focused on the plan's overall vision.

The sector managers work with the interdepartmental team for each sector to match plan recommendations with department resources. They encourage departments to fold plan recommendations into their work

Thanks to the neighborhood plan, the Delridge Neighborhoods Development Association was able to build the community's first library—the only Seattle library topped by affordable housing. Photograph by Ian Edelstein, City of Seattle; reprinted with permission.

plans. Department commitments are identified in Sector Implementation Plans written by the sector managers, so that progress can be monitored by the city and the community. In addition, the sector managers coordinate interdepartmental projects and leverage resources from the community, developers, foundations, and other agencies. As of 2002, this sector strategy had resulted in tens of millions of dollars' worth of transportation improvements, pedestrian lighting, affordable housing, community gardens, neighborhood-specific design guidelines, public art, human service programs, and public safety enhancements in accordance with neighborhood plans.

The second part of the implementation strategy was to generate additional resources by placing plan recommendations on the ballot in the form of bond and levy measures. Most plans called for enhanced library service, so the mayor and city council made that the focus of a 1998 bond measure. The voters approved it, resulting in twenty-seven new, expanded, or renovated branch libraries and a new downtown library designed by Pritzker Prize–winning architect Rem Koolhaus. Similarly, a 1999 levy is developing nine new or expanded community centers and two new Neighborhood Service Centers as requested in neighborhood plans. A 2000 levy provides funding for more than a hundred park and open space priorities: greenspace acquisition, athletic field improvements, pedestrian and bike trails, enhanced park maintenance, and expanded recreation programs for youths and seniors. All together, these bond and levy measures resulted in $470 million in additional funding, including $430 million specifically for plan implementation. The recent renewal of a low-income housing levy and a likely transportation levy will also support projects identified in the neighborhood plans. City officials have learned that citizens are willing to tax themselves for projects that they have requested.

The third part of the implementation strategy was to triple the Neighborhood Matching Fund from $1.5 million in 1998 to $4.5 million in 2001. About half of the money, plus the community's match, goes for projects recommended in the neighborhood plans. Besides helping to implement plans, the Matching Fund motivates citizens to stay involved after the planning by working on projects.

Thanks to Mayor Schell's three-part strategy, 1,220 plan recommendations had been implemented or were under way when he left office at the end of 2001. It was a good start, but much remains to be done to fully achieve the plans' goals by the target date of 2014. Whether the city continues to employ the sector strategy and whether plan implementation remains a high priority for the city will largely depend on the extent to which communities remain focused on their plans.

7

CELEBRATING COMMUNITY

Neighbor Appreciation Day

Celebrations have always been an important part of community life for Seattle neighborhoods and ethnic groups. In Southeast Seattle alone, seven neighborhood organizations built their own clubhouses during the first half of the twentieth century in order to have places to socialize. More recently, immigrants from the Philippines, Latin America, Laos, and Eritrea have developed community centers in Southeast Seattle. There are many such centers scattered throughout Seattle, but communities always manage to celebrate whether they have their own building or they use another venue such as a park facility, school, church, or the Seattle Center (which hosts eleven ethnic festivals each year) for the dances, concerts, films, dinners, or other events they sponsor.

Seasonal celebrations are especially popular. Ethnic communities celebrate their national holidays. Halloween and Christmas observances are organized by many neighborhood groups.

During the summer, most communities hold at least one large outdoor celebration. Sixteen ethnic and neighborhood festivals and parades take place in conjunction with the summer-long Seafair celebration, and other neighborhoods sponsor independent street fairs or multicultural festivals. Many neighborhoods celebrate summer, if not necessarily sunshine, with an annual day in the park, complete with barbecues, music, and games. In August, the National Night Out Against Crime draws about twenty thousand people to seven hundred block parties in neighborhoods throughout Seattle.

The Department of Neighborhoods plays a role in many of the celebrations. Neighborhood Service Center coordinators often assist event organizers with outreach and in obtaining permits. First-time festivals are eligible for support from the Neighborhood Matching Fund, and the completion of most Matching Fund projects prompts a celebration. Many community gatherings are held in P-Patch gardens. The department hosts an annual party to thank neighborhood activists. It also promotes one day each year when neighbors are encouraged to thank one another: Neighbor Appreciation Day.

Neighbor Appreciation Day can trace its origin to October 1994, when Mayor Rice visited Phinney Ridge on one of his regular neighborhood walking tours. Resident Judith Wood approached the mayor with a letter and asked him to read it personally. Mayor Rice opened the envelope on our drive back to city hall and intently read the letter first to himself and then out loud to me:

Dear Mayor Rice,

I would like to propose that a new citywide holiday be created in Seattle—Neighbor Appreciation Day. It has been my experience that my neighbors have greatly enhanced my quality of life in the city, and I believe this must be the case for other Seattle residents as well. I envision this holiday as a time to recognize and acknowledge the special relationships among neighbors, a time to say "thank you" for all that our neighbors have given us, both large and small.

My immediate neighbors sustain each other with front porch conversations, shared meals and backyard bounty, help with child care, loaned tools and work parties, and even the proverbial "borrowed" eggs. All this and more are given with a generosity of spirit that restores my faith in humanity. We are also lucky to have a vital community of neighbors in the form of the Phinney Neighborhood Association and other networks such as block watch, babysitting co-op, etc. All this makes me love my life in the city. This is what makes Seattle special for me.

I am convinced that neighborly feelings are not unique to my block or my part of Seattle. I am sure that caring neighbors are sustaining each other everywhere. I am tired of hearing about "bad" neighbors, lawsuits, and late night calls to the police. I cannot believe that is the norm. If it was, half the city would have left for a five-acre ranchette in the country by now and the other half would be shooting at each other.

Seattle, despite all its growth and changes, deserves its reputation as a wonderful place to live, and I believe that good relations between neighbors contribute significantly to this. Let's create a special day to celebrate the goodness in those around us and to reach out and strengthen our bonds to each other.

Sincerely,

Judith D. Wood

Mayor Rice handed the letter to me and asked me to work with Wood to plan a Neighbor Appreciation Day.

Initially, I was dubious about creating one more made-up holiday, even one called Neighbor Appreciation Day. At the mayor's direction, though, I met with Wood to learn why she felt it was so important. She told me that her proposal was in response to a recent newspaper article about a couple of feuding neighbors: the *Seattle Times* ran the story and encouraged readers to submit their own stories about "Neighbors from Hell." Wood objected to the newspaper highlighting the aberrant behavior of a few bad neighbors and, worse, ignoring what makes Seattle so special—its many, many caring neighbors. Caring neighbors should not be taken for granted, Wood declared; they should be thanked. A day to encourage and celebrate caring neighbors seemed obvious for Seattle, Wood continued. She had one final suggestion: the day should be observed in midwinter, the time of year when people tend to feel the most isolated.

Mayor Rice issued a proclamation designating the Saturday before Valentine's Day as Neighbor Appreciation Day. Its first observance was on February 11, 1995, and, from the first, it was truly a grassroots holiday. The Department of Neighborhoods did little beyond publicize the day and compile a calendar of community events. It was individuals and neighborhood organizations that seized the day and found their own ways to make it work for them. Neighbor Appreciation Day was well received that first year and has continued so each year since, becoming a tradition and growing larger every year.

The *Seattle Times* was a big help that first year. It publicized the new holiday and even invited readers to submit their own stories about good neighbors for the paper to publish on Neighbor Appreciation Day. When the newspaper was deluged with hundreds of powerful submittals, however, its editors decided to feature several good-neighbor stories each day during the week before the holiday.

An insurance company agreed to print greeting cards depicting caring neighbors. The first year's card was designed by a local greeting card company owned and operated by youths. In subsequent years, the Department of Neighborhoods sponsored a design contest open to all Seattle students. Hundreds of entries are submitted each year and the winners have ranged from a second grader to a high school senior. The selected artwork usually depicts diverse neighbors eating, playing, or working together. The inside of the card reads "Thank you, neighbor!" (An entry I especially liked, although it wasn't selected, showed then-President Clinton saying "Thanks, neighbor" to an extraterrestrial in a spaceship who was rescuing him from the roof of the White House.) The cards are available free of charge at all Neighborhood Service Centers so that people can write messages and deliver them to neighbors they want to thank. The print run for the cards has increased each year, but the number of cards made available for Neighbor Appreciation Day 2002—eighteen thousand—still wasn't enough to keep up with demand.

The heart of Neighbor Appreciation Day is its community events. Dozens are held each year, and I joined the mayor in getting to as many of them as possible. Usually, we started early in the morning, attending a pancake breakfast or two and then pitching in at a couple of neighborhood work parties before heading to Madrona for their celebration at 10:00 A.M.

The Madrona Community Council has sponsored a celebration every year from the start. Music, refreshments, and prominent speakers draw people to it, but the highlight is always the presentation of four Good Neighbor Awards. One goes to a local business or agency that has served the community especially well; the first year, a drug treatment program received the award. The second award recognizes the leader of a local neighborhood improvement project, and Madrona always has plenty of those to select from. The third award is for a

Charles McDade welcomes neighbors to the annual pancake breakfast sponsored by the Greater Madison Valley Community Council in celebration of Neighbor Appreciation Day. Photograph by Bradley Enghaus, Pacific Publishing; reprinted with permission.

Madrona resident who has contributed to the global community through his or her leadership on peace or justice initiatives. Public servants are thanked with the fourth award, which has gone to the local elementary school principal, police officers, firefighters, and even to me.

After visiting Madrona, the mayor and I would race to Laurelhurst for its 11:00 A.M. ceremony. Like the Madrona Community Council, the Laurelhurst Community Club has sponsored an award ceremony every year, but Laurelhurst's awards are more at the grassroots level. People in the community are invited to nominate a neighbor who has done something special for them, whether it was to welcome them to the neighborhood, pick up their children from school, walk their dog, make meals for them following surgery, or show other acts of kindness. Each nominee receives a certificate presented by the mayor; the nominators are acknowledged as well. More than twenty people received awards at the first ceremony. I was impressed that there were so many and I wondered if there would be anyone left to recognize the next year.

Amazingly, there have been at least that many people recognized each year since.

I remember the story of one recipient who had agreed to watch the house of his neighbor while the neighbor was on vacation. When this man checked on the house after a heavy rainstorm, he found that the basement had flooded. So he pumped the water out of the basement and then he dried out the contents, cleaned the carpet, and repainted the walls. This man's story, like those of the many other caring neighbors who were recognized in Laurelhurst, didn't have the kind of impact that would make the daily newspaper. Collectively, though, such stories describe the kind of mutual support that makes Seattle's neighborhoods the good places to live, work, and play that they are.

After visiting Laurelhurst, we would go to the next event, usually a neighborhood potluck, and from there, you name it: fire stations, schools, the Queen Anne Helpline, and the Ethiopian Community Center sponsored open houses for their neighbors; many block watch captains organized get-togethers in their homes; and always there were more work parties, shared meals, and recognition ceremonies. It wasn't unusual for me to participate in fifteen or sixteen events during the day. Every year, I would return home late at night, tired but inspired.

I got over being dubious about Neighbor Appreciation Day that first year. It quickly became, and I expect it always will be, my favorite holiday, because Neighbor Appreciation Day celebrates what makes Seattle so special.

8

MODELING COMMUNITY

Columbia City

One of the advantages that the Department of Neighborhoods brings to city government is that it enables an integrated approach to community development by focusing on whole neighborhoods rather than discrete functions. Paradoxically, in writing this book, I have described each of the department's programs separately in its own chapter in order to present the goals, mechanics, and outcomes of each program. It's important to understand how the programs interact, however, so this chapter describes that interaction in one neighborhood, Columbia City.

Columbia City traces its origin to 1890 with the construction of an electric railway running south from Seattle (comprising the current downtown) through Rainier Valley. The railway provided access to new sources of lumber for the rebuilding of Seattle after the Great Fire of 1889. The clearing of the land, combined with the new link to Seattle, made Rainier Valley an attractive location for development.

The initial development of Rainier Valley centered on the railway stops, one of which was being promoted with the name Columbia. By the time it was incorporated as a town in 1893, Columbia City boasted a lumber mill, town hall, school, post office, fraternal lodge, two churches, numerous stores, and a park. More stores, more churches, and the Hitts Fireworks Company followed. In 1907, Columbia City residents voted to become part of Seattle.

The character of this turn-of-the-century mill town, with its two- and three-story brick buildings, village green, and 1914 Carnegie library, remained largely intact through the years, so Columbia City was designated a landmark district in 1978. It is one of seven such districts now managed by the Historic Preservation program of the Department of Neighborhoods. A local Application Review Committee makes recommendations to the Landmarks Preservation Board, which must approve any exterior alterations to the more than forty commercial and residential buildings within the Columbia City Landmark District; the district's streets, sidewalks, and park also are protected. As a result, the physical appearance of Columbia City, with its small-town atmosphere, has been preserved.

Behind the historic facades, though, the neighborhood was in decline in the 1970s. Several longtime businesses closed, and only the taverns seemed to thrive. The community had to fight to keep pornographic films out of the local theater and to force the Seattle School District to replace the roof of Columbia Elementary School, which leaked into buckets interspersed with the students' desks. The historic district designation and a new streetscape installed by the city were encouraging, but they were insufficient to attract new retail activity. At night, the new sidewalks were often the scene of drug dealing and prostitution.

The decline of Columbia City continued into the 1990s. Gang violence and graffiti were becoming more prevalent, along with drug dealing and prostitution. Both of the neighborhood's clothing stores, the theater, and the furniture store had closed, and finally, the neighborhood's only supermarket went out of business. Several restaurants remained open, but their ownership continually changed. Some storefronts had bars on the windows and others were boarded up.

Increasingly, the legitimate activities in Columbia City centered on government. The post office, elementary school, library, community center, and Neighborhood Service Center became the "anchor businesses." The Service Center, for instance, grew to attract more than fifty thousand customers a year for public utility payments, municipal court hearings, pet licenses, bus passes, passport applications, and other services.

The foot traffic generated by the Neighborhood Service Center helped keep Columbia City viable, but it was the center's coordinator— first Ron Angeles, then Ellen Broeske, and finally Pamela Green—who played a key role in the revitalization of the surrounding businesses.

The coordinator helped organize the Columbia City Merchants Association and brought it together with the Columbia City Neighborhood Association and other community interests to discuss strategies for revitalization. A frequent forum for these discussions was the Southeast District Council, which the coordinator helped establish in 1988.

As described in chapter 6, the Southeast District Council undertook a neighborhood planning process in 1990. The resulting plan convinced the city to build a large, new Rainier Community Center in Columbia City, and the plan also generated many ideas that the community carried out with the coordinator's assistance. Like the plan itself, most of those projects were supported by the Neighborhood Matching Fund.

ENERGIZING THE COMMUNITY CENTER

The Rainier Community Center, like the other twenty-five community centers in Seattle, relies heavily on its recreation advisory council of volunteers to develop and raise money for the center's programs, including a wide variety of cultural and recreational classes for all ages. Much of the center's programming and its surrounding athletic fields involve youth basketball, baseball, football, and soccer teams managed and coached by volunteers. When the old Rainier Community Center was replaced with a facility more than twice its size in order to better serve the community's high concentration of children, more programs and more volunteers were needed to fill it. A group of mothers took advantage of the opportunity and used the Neighborhood Matching Fund to develop an indoor playground so that their young children (and they themselves) could continue to exercise and socialize during the long rainy season. Similarly, the Rainier Community Center became the home of Project Compute, an award-winning computer instruction program for youth, developed and led by a local volunteer; this Boeing Company employee also used the Neighborhood Matching Fund to produce an engineering curriculum for youth.

Other community members initiated Matching Fund projects to improve the grounds surrounding the new community center. Dozens of trees were planted over the course of several years in the adjacent park and around the athletic fields.

Our son and daughter played on the local baseball and softball teams, so Sarah managed a project to redevelop the three substandard fields. The high school team members joined with their parents to demolish and remove the old backstops, fences, and bleachers. Sheets of plywood waiting to be painted filled our backyard over the summer and provided material for nervous speculation about what it was that we were building: there was probably a collective sigh of relief among our neighbors when we finally hauled the painted lumber to the ball field for the construction of dugouts. The ball field project gave me direct knowledge of how much work it takes to coordinate such projects, and it also gave me a tremendous sense of camaraderie and pride. We no longer felt embarrassed when we hosted the suburban teams.

CONNECTING SCHOOL AND NEIGHBORHOOD

The Rainier Community Center was one neighborhood locus of youth activity, and the other was the local school, three blocks southwest. The ties between Columbia Elementary School and the neighborhood had been severed during the desegregation program. Although mandatory busing had ended, the disconnectedness continued because the neighborhood school was replaced by Orca, an alternative elementary school with a citywide draw. Both the school and the neighborhood were eager to reestablish a connection for their mutual benefit, so together they turned to the Neighborhood Matching Fund for support.

The first joint project between the Columbia City Neighborhood Association and the Orca Parent Teacher Association was the development of a community garden in 1990. Volunteers built thirty-inch-high raised beds on the large asphalt lot at the east end of the school and decorated them with ceramic tiles made by the students. The garden, marked by Worm Crossing signs, serves as an outdoor classroom for the students and is part of their environmental curriculum. Community members assist the students with their gardening and, during the summer, maintain the gardens for their own use.

One project led to another. In 1992, parents and neighbors added a large greenhouse to the garden and later created a wildlife sanctuary. Recently, volunteers removed much of the asphalt on the west end of

Students and teachers tend the garden at Orca Elementary School. Photograph by Ian Edelstein, City of Seattle; reprinted with permission.

the school and replaced it with landscaping, play equipment, and art so that the school property now is much better integrated with the village green across the street.

During the same time, Orca and three nearby elementary schools collaborated with the Columbia City Neighborhood Association and Mount Baker Community Club to plan an innovative community school program: Powerful Schools. The program began in 1992 with each school being open a different night of the week as a venue for community members to learn from one another. Classes have been offered on bicycle repair, gardening, cooking, martial arts, gymnastics, hip-hop, earthquake preparedness, geology, and a host of other topics. My wife and daughter took a sign language class with neighbors of all ages, many ethnicities, and the full spectrum of hearing abilities. Diversity like that is the rule rather than the exception with Powerful Schools night classes.

Along with inviting the community into its facilities in the evening, Powerful Schools welcomes community volunteers during the school day. Local artists and writers work with teachers and with students through the Powerful Arts program and the Powerful Writers program. Powerful Buddies pairs caring neighbors with students who need the benefit of a positive role model. First and second graders who are at risk for reading failure get individual assistance from specially trained volunteers in the Powerful Readers program. Other volunteers provide tutoring in the homework center. Powerful Schools also pays some low-income parents to work as tutors and teachers' aides, an experience that benefits both the parents and the children.

In 1993, Powerful Schools used the Neighborhood Matching Fund to open a Grassroots Technology Center, where parents can learn computer skills from their children. The center serves as a place where everyone can have access to a computer whether or not they can afford to own one. Low-income families can even earn their own refurbished computer by attending a day-long class in basic computer skills. Upgrades can be earned by providing child care, transporting computers, or otherwise supporting the program.

Powerful Schools is all about partnerships. Both community and school clearly benefit from their symbiotic relationship. And each school gains by being associated with the other three: the schools share their strengths with one another and the staff participate in joint training. Every year, Powerful Schools celebrates these partnerships with its Night at the Rap, a performance at a downtown concert hall showcasing the best musical talent from all four schools.

IMPROVING LIVES BY FIXING BIKES

Half a block east of Orca is a business where most of the workers are children. The business, a nonprofit organization known as Bike Works, got its start through the Neighborhood Matching Fund in 1996.

Bike Works benefits the community in several ways. Most pragmatically, it's the only bicycle repair shop in Southeast Seattle and it charges low rates. Furthermore, the business occupies a formerly vacant and blighted storefront that was renovated by community volunteers. Most important, the business nourishes youth by providing them with a positive place to spend time, opportunities for exercise, a way to build self-esteem, exposure to community service, and the development of job skills and technical skills.

Anyone between the ages of nine and seventeen is eligible to participate in the Earn-a-Bike program. The kids attend eight classes in bicycle repair. Then they go to work repairing used bicycles that have been donated to Bike Works. After completing twenty-four hours of work, each is given a refurbished bicycle, a helmet, and a lock. So far, more than 150 kids have earned bicycles. So many bicycles have been refurbished that they are donated to organizations supporting foster children and homeless adults. Recently, five hundred recycled bicycles were shipped to Ghana.

Bike Works also sponsors regular rodeos at which bicycle safety is taught. Bike Works organized the Street Burners bicycle club and frequently leads neighborhood rides, lending bicycles to whoever needs them. Bike Works also manages an annual Kids Bike Swap at which children can trade up to replace a bicycle they've outgrown. All of this is made possible by a small staff and about a hundred adult volunteers.

CELEBRATING DIVERSITY

Columbia City refers to itself as the Neighborhood of Nations. Its population is about a third Asian, a third black, and a third white. Dozens of languages are spoken in this neighborhood that is home to many recent immigrants from Southeast Asia, East Africa, Eastern Europe, and Central America. The neighborhood also has a large gay and lesbian community. Many regard this diversity as Columbia City's greatest asset, so the local organizations looked for ways to highlight it.

When the Christian Science Church closed in 1994, SouthEast Effective Development (the local community development corporation) and the Rainier Chamber of Commerce (the business association for the entire district) joined forces to reopen the building as the Rainier Valley Cultural Center. They turned to the Neighborhood Matching Fund for help in purchasing and restoring this prominent landmark. The basement was renovated to serve as a museum for the Rainier Valley Historical Society, which has developed several exhibits with support from the Matching Fund. The church sanctuary was converted into a theater that hosts a wide range of performing artists, including the Rainier Valley Youth Theater. In 2001, the Matching Fund helped sponsor four artists who came from Cuba for the summer to teach the youth drama, music, and dance; the result was a powerful theater production based on Cuba's East African traditions.

The Rainier Valley Cultural Center is located on the village green that links it with Orca School to the south and the library to the east. A large Native American whale fin sculpture stands in the middle of the park—another Matching Fund–supported project. In 1993, the Rainier Chamber staged the first annual Rainier Valley Heritage Festival in the park. That two-day event celebrated the community's multiethnic heritage with an array of food, exhibits, music, and dance. The Matching Fund helped launch the festival, and the Neighborhood Service Center coordinator continues to support the festival by providing essential outreach and logistics. She provides similar assistance with events at the Rainier Valley Cultural Center and with many of the other projects described in this chapter.

UNITING EAST AFRICANS AROUND COMPUTERS

The growing East African community was eager for access to computers. Computers could enable them to stay in touch with their homeland, to learn English, to search for jobs, and to do whatever else people use computers for. Due to language barriers, though, the computers at Orca and at the Rainier Community Center weren't meeting the community's needs. The East African community decided to establish its own computer center with support from the Neighborhood Matching Fund.

In 2000, the Horn of Africa Computer Center opened in rented office space in Columbia City. The center serves immigrants and refugees from Djibouti, Eritrea, Ethiopia, and Somalia. Computer classes and the computers' software and hardware are geared to the languages of Amharic,

Oromo, Somali, and Tigrinya. These different languages, like the countries' contested borders, are the cause of fighting within East Africa, but, at the Horn of Africa Computer Center, East African Seattleites share the common objective of learning computers and succeeding in their new country.

REVITALIZING THE BUSINESS DISTRICT

Although the projects described thus far in this chapter have contributed much to Columbia City's quality of life, none of them was specifically intended to revitalize the business district. Faced with continuing business closures, a group of residents and merchants organized themselves as the Columbia City Revitalization Committee in 1995. They sought the help of Cheryl Cronander, the Department of Neighborhoods staff person who was coordinating implementation of the Southeast Seattle Action Plan.

Using the department's connections around the city, Cronander invited leaders of successful revitalization efforts in other business districts to share their strategies with the Columbia City group. She also arranged for economists, realtors, developers, architects and other experts to advise the group on how to strengthen existing businesses and attract new ones. The best thing she did, though, was to encourage the group to develop its own strategies based on the neighborhood's assets and the community's interests. What she proposed was a town meeting using an "open space" format to identify revitalization projects and the people to carry them out.

The first International Pancake Breakfast and Town Meeting was held on a Saturday morning in the spring of 1995 at the Tropicana, a Filipino restaurant and bakery. The free food lured a diverse crowd of about 150 people who filled every chair and all of the aisle space. After breakfast, everyone was asked to think of a project that could improve Columbia City. If it was an idea an individual felt passionately about, that person was invited to summarize the project in a few words on a large sheet of paper and to take a couple of minutes to describe the idea to the entire assembly. Once everyone had an opportunity to share ideas, the papers summarizing all of the proposed projects were posted in the front of the room, with similar ideas grouped together. Each cluster of ideas was then assigned to an individual restaurant or store in the neighborhood.

At that point, all town meeting participants voted with their feet by joining a discussion of whatever idea most appealed to them. The project originator was responsible for leading the discussion. Participants were encouraged to feel free to leave one discussion and join another until they found a project and a group that resonated with them. Only the ideas that stimulated sufficient interest were pursued because there was no one else to carry them out. By the end of the morning, six projects had been launched and each group had planned its initial steps, assigned tasks, and scheduled its next meeting.

The town meeting worked so well that it has become an annual event. As many as two hundred people have attended, so the venue switched to the larger Royal Esquire Club, a gathering place for African American men. The town meetings continue to generate exciting new ideas, and they also celebrate the many successful projects that have resulted from previous meetings.

The biggest success to come out of that first town meeting was proposed by Darryl Smith, who later became president of the Columbia City Revitalization Committee. Smith's idea was to create an event that would showcase the neighborhood's ethnic restaurants and give the community a sense of what a vibrant Columbia City would look like by enticing crowds of people to patronize the restaurants on a single night. A $5 cover charge allowed people to see five different live music performances in five restaurants: Ethiopian, Filipino, Italian, and Thai restaurants plus a Victorian tearoom operated by an African American couple. The initial event attracted three hundred people, filling Columbia City's sidewalks with happy customers and putting smiles on the faces of the restaurateurs as well. It was such a success that Beatwalk has become a regular event on the first Friday of each month. There are many more customers now, and there are eleven venues, but the cover charge is still $5.

Beatwalk was so effective in attracting customers to Columbia City that Karen Kinney came to the second town meeting to propose adding another attraction: a farmers' market. Meeting participants loved

Orca Elementary School students sell plant starts from their garden at the Columbia City Farmers' Market. Photograph by Bradley Enghaus, Pacific Publishing; reprinted with permission.

Kinney's idea and worked with her over the next two years to plan and organize it. The Columbia City Farmers' Market opened in June 1998. Ironically, the venue was the large parking lot surrounding the neighborhood's former supermarket. That first farmers' market featured more than thirty growers selling fresh, locally grown produce, much of it organic. Live music and cooking demonstrations contributed to a festive atmosphere. Literature tables provided information on current community issues and projects. The roughly 1,500 people who turned out every Wednesday from June through October seemed to enjoy the opportunity to visit with neighbors as much as they enjoyed buying directly from producers. Each year the market has attracted more vendors and more customers—in 2002, an average of about 2,500 a day. Surveys show that most of the customers, when they have finished at the farmers' market for the day, stay to shop or eat elsewhere in the business district.

Columbia City residents use some Hollywood magic to transform their business district. Photograph by Jim Diers.

Many other equally successful projects have been born at the town meetings. Columbia City now has an annual garden tour and an annual barbecue cook-off. Two handsome kiosks were installed along the sidewalk to promote those and other events: the kiosks incorporate panels with historic photographs of Columbia City. The unkempt parking strip next to the farmers' market has been converted into a beautiful garden. Used holiday decorations from other business districts were refurbished for display in Columbia City.

Even with these and many other projects and with the marketing efforts of the Columbia City Revitalization Committee, a half-block in this historic district remained boarded up and vacant as it had been for twenty years. Finally, at one town meeting, someone suggested that if the community couldn't attract real businesses, they could at least pretend. The community used the Neighborhood Matching Fund to contract with the SouthEast Seattle Arts Council to paint murals depicting businesses on the plywood covering the doors and windows. They painted an ice cream parlor on the corner and next to that a bookstore, toy store, hat shop, and dance studio. Suddenly, Columbia City seemed to be reborn. The murals looked so realistic that passing motorists sometimes stopped to shop. The murals also captured the imagination of a developer and several business owners. Within a year, every one of the murals had to be removed because real businesses wanted to locate there. That half-block is now home to an Italian delicatessen, a pub, and a cooperative art gallery, which is yet another project that has resulted from a town meeting.

PLANNING FOR THE FUTURE

When Columbia City was identified as one of thirty-seven neighborhoods targeted for growth in the city's Comprehensive Plan, those attending the 1996 town meeting decided to form a committee to begin work on a neighborhood plan. The committee hired consultants with funding from the Neighborhood Planning Office and conducted an extensive outreach process. They interviewed fifty business owners and sent out surveys to residents, of which 422 were returned. The planning committee organized a speakers bureau to communicate with hard-to-reach groups, including non-English-speaking groups. The planning committee also sponsored a project in which youth photographed local problem places and described how they thought the places could be improved. All of this input was used to develop recommendations that were later discussed in public meetings and revised accordingly. The draft plan was presented at a community-wide validation event at which participants voted on the recommendations. In February 1999, three years later, the plan was completed. It included recommendations for strengthening the business district, developing additional housing, enhancing public safety, and designing the proposed light rail line and local station in a way that would contribute to the plan's other objectives.

The Department of Neighborhoods' Southeast Sector manager then began working with the Columbia City Revitalization Committee and other city departments to implement the plan. The city council approved zoning changes to restrict the scale of development around the historic district and to add capacity for residential development elsewhere along the neighborhood's two major arterials. The former site of the Hitts Fireworks Company was purchased to preserve 2.8 wooded acres for public use. Voters approved funding to expand the Columbia City library. Curbs and planting strips were installed along a residential street. In addition to these city actions, the community began work on several projects of its own to help implement the plan.

Columbia City has indeed been revitalized. Longtime businesses like Bob's Meats and Matthieson's Flowers are flourishing. Many new businesses have opened in the past decade: six new restaurants, three clothing stores, two coffee shops, two art galleries, two theaters, a Somali grocery, a bicycle shop, a locksmith, a lighting fixture store, a pet shop, and a mailing service. Vacant storefronts? Not in Columbia City.

When the San Francisco Chamber of Commerce chose Seattle as the site of its annual intercity visit in 2000, they spent half a day in Columbia City. Eighty of San Francisco's elected officials, CEOs, and other civic leaders toured Orca Elementary, Bike Works, the Cultural Center, the Southeast Neighborhood Service Center, and the business district. They marveled at the extraordinary level of community involvement and called Columbia City "a world-class neighborhood"—an apt description and quite a change from ten years earlier!

9

REPLICATING NEIGHBORHOOD PROGRAMS

S eattle's Department of Neighborhoods certainly did not invent the idea of city government partnering with its communities. We built on the foundation of Seattle's Little City Halls and P-Patch Program, which started in the early 1970s. We also learned a great deal from cities like Portland, Oregon, and St. Paul, Minnesota, which truly were pioneers in developing neighborhood programs.

Representatives of many cities tell me that they are now learning from the experience of Seattle's Department of Neighborhoods. They are interested in the new approaches we took to empowering communities and helping city government as a whole be more responsive to neighborhoods. The Neighborhood Matching Fund, Neighborhood Service Centers, P-Patch, and neighborhood planning and implementation programs are especially popular models. Dozens of cities are replicating one or more Department of Neighborhoods programs.

Few people argue with the concept of participatory democracy, but a number of cities balk at moving in a direction similar to Seattle's. Following are three basic, and understandable, reservations that I hear repeatedly, and my responses to them.

"THIS ISN'T SEATTLE"

Everywhere I show my slides and tell stories of community self-help efforts, someone invariably says, "That's wonderful, Jim, but this isn't Seattle," or words to that effect. The difference seems obvious when I'm in a small town like Shasta Lake, California, or Langsford, British Columbia, or in a big city like New York or Paris. But I also hear it in cities like Baltimore, Cleveland, Wichita, or Salt Lake City; cities where, people note, communities are organized in different ways, and have different interests and issues, than in Seattle.

Sometimes I'm the one who points out that Seattle is different. I received a call from a suburban mayor who said, "Jim, I love what you're doing. How can I organize my own department of neighborhoods?"

My initial thought was, "First you need neighborhoods. Maybe you could organize a department of cul-de-sacs." Fortunately, I kept my thoughts to myself. What I said was, "First you need to identify where community comes together in your city."

I believe that people everywhere yearn for community, even in the suburbs. Enrique Penalosa, formerly mayor of Bogota, Colombia, and currently living in suburban New York, told me that his observations have led him to conclude that suburbanites go to malls not so much to shop as to be with other people. Indeed, Ron Sher has incorporated community activities into his shopping centers in suburban Seattle; the stage at Third Place Books in Lake Forest Park is programmed by a nonprofit organization of five hundred neighbors. Malls, schools, and churches often substitute for neighborhoods as places where community comes together.

Elected officials, like community organizers, need to start where people are and build their programs of community empowerment accordingly. Bellevue and Everett in Washington and San Antonio, Texas, have established their little city halls in the malls. In Columbus, Ohio, twenty Citizen Service Centers are set up in churches, schools, and recreation centers during the city's Pride Week.

Some cities can't relate to all of the park, garden, and other environmental projects undertaken by community groups in Seattle. That's okay. The neighborhood matching fund concept is not inherently biased toward environmental projects. It's intended to support whatever is a particular community's priority. A matching fund could be used to paint and repair the homes of low-income seniors, improve facades in blighted business districts, install traffic circles, post neighborhood identification signs, paint murals, renovate public facilities, build ball fields—it's up to the community to decide how to use the fund within whatever parameters are set by local government. Likewise, local conditions should determine which groups are eligible to apply. Faith-based organizations and service clubs are ineligible in Seattle, but they could well be eligible elsewhere.

Programs similar to Seattle's have, in fact, been established in a wide variety of places. There are neighborhood matching fund programs in Victoria, British Columbia; Shoreline, Washington; Eugene, Oregon; Santa Monica, California; Salt Lake City, Utah; Las Vegas, Nevada; Wichita, Kansas; Houston, Texas; Madison, Wisconsin; Detroit, Michigan; Cleveland, Ohio; Buffalo, New York; Sarasota, Florida; Port Elizabeth, South Africa; and dozens of other cities. Facilities similar to Seattle's Neighborhood Service Centers can be found in places as different as San Diego, California; Jefferson Parish, Louisiana; Baltimore, Maryland; and Nante, France.

"WHAT ABOUT THE NIMBYS?"

No one comes right out and says, "We don't trust the people," but what I do hear constantly is, "What about the NIMBYs?" NIMBY stands for Not In My Back Yard, whether the undesired object is an airport, a landfill, a jail, increased density, low-income housing, or a human service agency. NIMBY can describe self-centered individuals, but it is often used to characterize neighborhoods in general. Public officials like to invoke the acronym to explain why they don't try to empower neighborhoods to develop their own plans.

I deny such characterizations of whole neighborhoods. While I admit that some individuals are narrow-minded, I have come to trust the community, especially when the community organizations are broadly based, democratic, and empowered. I believe that people act responsibly to the extent that they are given responsibility. It is when people know they have no power that communities take extreme positions, expecting their positions to be moderated by the decision makers. NIMBYs are usually the product of centralized decision making, especially when officials try to sneak a project past the community and impose one-size-fits-all solutions regardless of local conditions.

Low-income communities are the favorite target for siting unpopular projects. Lower real estate costs are one reason. Another reason is that low-income communities often have less power to say no. That was certainly true of Southeast Seattle prior to 1976.

With the founding of the South End Seattle Community Organization (SESCO), for which I worked, the community became more particular about what came into its neighborhood. We wanted our community to be treated equitably, and as a result we were often maligned as NIMBYs.

I believe that SESCO's intervention resulted in better outcomes for Seattle as a whole. SESCO's opposition to garbage incinerators being constructed in the community led to a model recycling program. When the city wanted to build an animal shelter in Georgetown's residential neighborhood, SESCO successfully demanded that it be sited in a more central, industrial part of town. The organization's campaign against a condominium development saved a large Japanese garden, which has since become a cherished park. When SESCO's protests stopped pornographic films from taking over the community's only theater, everyone (except the pornographer) was better off. On these occasions, we wore our NIMBY label as a badge of honor.

I was less comfortable being called a NIMBY neighborhood, however, when SESCO opposed additional low-income housing in the community. It was no fun to be identified as a critic of low-income housing. It was also unfair, since Southeast Seattle had the highest concentration of subsidized housing in the city. SESCO successfully advocated that additional low-income housing be dispersed throughout all of Seattle.

SESCO's objection was not to having low-income people as neighbors; the objection was to having housing in the community that was controlled by people outside the community. Southeast Seattle's experience was that absentee landlords led to substandard housing conditions, escalating rents, and a lack of security that kept most tenants transient: it's difficult to build a sense of community with a population that is constantly in flux. Publicly owned housing had similar problems because it was concentrated in large complexes that were not integrated with the rest of the community.

Today, subsidized housing is being developed in Southeast Seattle by community-based organizations. HomeSight is building houses and townhouses for first-time homebuyers. Not only do those homes fit with the character of the neighborhood, but homeownership gives the low-income residents a stake in the community. SouthEast Effective Development is building and renovating apartment buildings to provide quality housing; it also trains tenants to manage the housing themselves. Even the Seattle Housing Authority is doing its part by using federal Hope VI funding to redevelop its two large, low-income "garden communities" so that low- and middle-income residents live side-by-side in similar housing. Not a word has been heard from NIMBYs.

As I mentioned in chapter 6, the biggest reservation about empowering neighborhoods to develop their own plans was that NIMBY attitudes would lead to down-zoning to allow less density. What actually happened, however, was that no loss of zoning capacity resulted from the planning process and two neighborhoods even called for higher growth targets. Being empowered enabled communities to focus their energy on how to make growth work for their neighborhoods rather than on fighting externally generated plans for growth. The experience of Seattle has repeatedly proven that the best way to counter NIMBY attitudes is to empower the community.

"WE CAN'T AFFORD IT"

At a time when local government has more responsibilities than revenue, many cities contend that they can't afford to take on new programs, especially if those programs are outside the realm of traditional mandates such as public safety and transportation. I contend that cities can't afford *not* to fund neighborhood programs, given the many additional resources that those programs leverage. Seattle's Neighborhood Matching Fund more than doubles the value of the city's investment. The neighborhood planning program leveraged $470 million in new tax revenues. And those figures don't even begin to account for the tremendous value inherent in building a stronger sense of community and a citizenry that is more engaged with its government. Before I get too carried away, though, I have to acknowledge that none of these arguments carries any weight if government has no spare money to leverage.

A more realistic response to the concern about too little money is the same advice that I give to neighborhood leaders: "Think big, start small." Officials in other cities get cold feet when I tell them that Seattle's Department of Neighborhoods has a hundred staff members and an annual budget of $12 million. I hasten to add that Seattle's neighborhood programs began thirty years ago. We started small and have grown over time.

There is more than one way to start small. One way is to begin with a single program as Seattle did when it initiated little city halls in the early 1970s. Another way is to limit the size of each program. Since many cities have found a neighborhood matching fund a good place to start, I will illustrate with that.

No city needs Seattle's $4.5 million a year to operate a matching fund program. Los Angeles, California, has the second largest program at $600,000 and Charlotte, North Carolina, is next with $300,000. Duluth, Minnesota, and St. Petersburg, Florida, are close behind. Most cities' matching funds, though, have an annual budget of $50,000 or less. That money goes a long way because most programs cap their project awards at $5,000 or less—even in Los Angeles. In Savannah, Georgia, a Grants for Blocks program that was initiated in 1993 limits awards to $500. That kind of mini-grant program is being replicated in a number of cities.

Another way to start small is to limit what kinds of projects are eligible. In Vancouver, British Columbia, the matching fund is managed by the Parks Board, so only park-related projects can apply. The matching fund in Lantana, Florida, can be used only for housing rehabilitation.

Other cities have programs that limit eligibility to specific communities. The Los Angeles program started in a single council district before expanding citywide. In many cities, only low-income neighborhoods are eligible because the funding comes from the federal Community Development Block Grant.

It is also possible to operate a matching fund program without tapping government revenues at all. In Columbus, Ohio, the matching fund is sponsored by the private Columbus Foundation. Likewise, in Seattle, the success of the Department of Neighborhoods' program has inspired foundations (e.g., the Seattle Foundation and South Downtown Foundation) and corporations (e.g., Washington Insurance Council and Starbucks) as well as other government jurisdictions (e.g., Puget Sound Urban

Resources Partnership, King County, and other city departments including Parks, Transportation, Utilities, and Information Technology) to establish their own matching fund programs. There is a growing recognition among foundations, corporations, and government agencies nationwide that funding is better appreciated and goes farther when it supports community-driven projects.

As illustrated by the preceding examples of the Neighborhood Matching Fund and Neighborhood Service Centers, there are many ways that Seattle's programs could be tailored to fit the unique character and resources of communities and their governments in other locations. This sort of adaptation is critical to successful replication. Just as Seattle liberally adapted the ideas it borrowed from cities such as Portland and St. Paul, no jurisdiction should adopt Seattle's programs wholesale. While I hope that my descriptions of the mechanics of Seattle's programs have some value, my more fervent wish is that my stories will inspire others to make a similar commitment to empowering their communities in whatever ways make the most sense for them. I have no desire to franchise Seattle's Department of Neighborhoods. What I do want is to get more people in more places more involved in their communities and more involved in decisions that affect their own and their neighbors' lives.

10

CONCLUSION

T his is a book that people urged me for a long time to write. Government officials and community activists in many cities requested a manual to help them replicate Seattle's programs. University professors suggested a case study so that they can compare Seattle's approach to that of other cities. And Mayor Paul Schell frequently encouraged me to produce a coffee table book filled with stories and photographs of the many inspiring community projects.

It was Mayor-elect Greg Nickels, though, who finally gave me the incentive and the time to write this book. He fired me. The date was December 13, 2001. I don't think he knew that it was my birthday. In fact, I like to think that he didn't know me very well at all.

The reaction to my being fired was overwhelming. Nickels's surprise move was greeted by hundreds of letters of protest, critical press coverage, a unanimous Seattle City Council resolution proclaiming Jim Diers Day, and community activists joining forces under the banner of "Neighborhoods Rock!" to advocate for the future of the Department of Neighborhoods. I was deluged with e-mail messages, cards, phone calls, and people stopping me on the street, many of them complete strangers, thanking me for the difference that the department had made in their lives.

I also heard from people in other cities, including Linda Campbell, Manager of Community Services in Shellharbour, Australia. Her e-mail read: "I hope this change brings you opportunities to share your skills with an even broader base and lots more communities are able to benefit from your experience with neighbourhood plans and other wonderful

When the city council proclaimed Jim Diers Day, I saluted the activists and co-workers who have made the Department of Neighborhoods so successful. Photograph by Renee C. Byer, © 2002, Seattle Post-Intelligencer; *reprinted with permission.*

neighbourhood initiatives. The City of Seattle is a leader in community and neighbourhood development not just in the U.S. but as far away as Shellharbour! Good luck, Jim, and if there is a book in the pipeline, I'll be ordering an early copy." That was the clincher. I realized that now, finally, I would have time to write that book.

LESSONS LEARNED

I have tried to include something for everyone in this book about Seattle's Department of Neighborhoods—program details for other cities, a literature review for the academicians, and stories and photographs for Mayor Schell. Yet, my purpose in writing this book is less to promote particular programs and projects than it is to inspire public officials, students, and people in general to help build strong communities. There are many routes to community empowerment, and each community needs to find its own way. My hope is that by sharing the lessons I have learned on my own journey, I can make it easier for others to find paths that work for them. Because these lessons are scattered throughout the book and some were not included at all, I will conclude by summarizing what I have learned about community, community organizing, community initiatives, and the role of government.

The first lesson I learned is that a neighborhood is not the same as a community. A neighborhood is a geographic area that people share, while a community is a group of people who identify with and support one another. It is possible for a neighborhood to lack a strong sense of community, and conversely, it is possible for there to be a strong sense of community among people who don't share a neighborhood. A community can be defined by a common culture, language, or sexual orientation, regardless of geography.

Strong communities are those that rely on their own resources, including the assets that each and every person possesses. As the Eritrean Association of Greater Seattle puts it, "Our mission is guided by our shared vision that each member, from the youngest to the most senior, has a need to be cared for and nurtured and at the same time each one has the ability and the responsibility to contribute back to the community."

Individual reciprocity is not sufficient, however. Communities are most powerful when they take collective action. The process of building that kind of power is called community organizing.

The key to community organizing is to start where the people are. The more local the activity, the higher the percentage of people who will get involved. Starting where people are, however, also means respecting their sense of community, whether or not it is tied to geography. It further entails building on existing networks. Most people are already organized and cannot reasonably be expected to develop an entirely new set of relationships and find time for yet another organization.

Starting where people are also involves identifying their interests. That does not mean promoting a cause and seeing who follows; that means listening. The organizer should be prepared to hear and understand interests that may differ from her or his own. If a common interest involves an issue, that issue should be framed in a way that is as immediate, as specific, and as achievable as possible. People get involved to the extent that they can have an impact on the things they care about. Community plans, projects, and social events are other good ways to bring people together. Whatever the approach, whatever the issue, it is best to think big and start small.

One good place to start is with community-initiated planning, which can have numerous advantages over planning conducted by institutions. Many more people are motivated to get involved. Local knowledge and values are incorporated. A more holistic approach is generally taken. And the resulting plan is much more likely to be implemented. This assumes, of course, that the planning process is inclusive and that it is coordinated with neighboring plans.

Likewise, community self-help projects tend to have qualities that are missing in projects generated by institutions. Innovations are more likely to emanate from community efforts. Communities have a knack for converting a problem into an asset, whether it is a graffiti-covered wall, a vacant lot, an abandoned building, a dead tree, garden waste, fallen apples, discarded bicycles, a wet ball field, a stagnant pond, a broken pipe, or incessant rain. Communities design and build some of the best-loved public spaces, which in turn build a stronger sense of community. A good example is community gardens, which are also a tremendous tool for conducting environmental education and feeding the hungry. If the community is involved in producing public art (and why else would it be called public?), the art will probably reflect the community's character and values and be integrated with the fabric of the neighborhood. People tend to respect and maintain community projects.

Community initiatives generally have a positive effect on the environment. While academicians struggle to define and measure *sustainability,* strong communities tend to practice sustainability whether or not they have ever heard of the term. In communities, people care for one another and the place they share. Just as they value heritage, communities are mindful of future generations. They are also more self-sufficient and less reliant on outside resources. "Meeting present needs without jeopardizing future resources" is not only a common definition of sustainability; it is the goal of empowered communities.

Community school programs exemplify the creative use of resources that would otherwise go to waste. School facilities are typically under-utilized on evenings and weekends and during summers. Yet school gymnasiums, libraries, computer centers, theaters, woodshops, kitchens, classrooms, playgrounds, and parking lots could be put to good use by the community. Neighbors with skills, knowledge, and time to share, meanwhile, are generally overlooked by the schools. By fully utilizing the resources of both communities and schools, community school programs benefit students and neighbors alike.

Strong communities can also play a major role in crime prevention. Too many block watch programs focus on encouraging residents to install deadbolt locks and peer through their peepholes for suspicious behavior by outsiders. Real security comes from opening doors to community life. No amount of public safety spending can buy the kind of security that comes from neighbors caring and watching out for one another.

Community initiatives such as these are essential as local government revenues fail to keep pace with increasingly complex social and environmental issues. Government can be a catalyst for community initiatives, but to do so, it must first change some bad habits. Too many local governments treat citizens as nothing more than customers; citizens, in turn, think of themselves only as taxpayers; government resources, consequently, continue to decline. All local governments have citizen participation processes, but most of them are a charade. As Daniel Kemmis wrote about public hearings, "The one element that is almost totally lacking is anything that might be characterized as 'public hearing.'"

Government must learn to see neighborhoods not only as places with great needs, but as communities with tremendous resources. Communities can do so much that government cannot, and working together, communities and government can do even more that could not be done otherwise. For example, citizens are willing to tax themselves for projects and programs that their communities request. Government can tap these resources to the extent that it respects the wisdom of the community and acts more as a facilitator than as an expert. It can provide tools and resources for community initiatives, but government should never do for community organizations what they can do for themselves.

Community organizations dependent on government for their legitimacy and support are not community organizations at all.

Government programs intended to build strong communities should not be ghettoized within the bureaucracy. The best programs are those that help all government departments engage with the community. Gaining the participation of other departments (and elected officials) requires listening to their concerns, identifying their self-interests, building relationships, and giving them credit. Government workers are often as frustrated with the bureaucracy as are the citizens they seek to help, and community-centered partnerships can help liberate them from their bureaucratic constraints.

QUESTIONS REMAINING

When Mayor-elect Nickels fired me, my own liberation from the bureaucracy left me with mixed emotions. I realized how fortunate I had been to be part of the Department of Neighborhoods under three different mayors, and I looked forward to the opportunity of exploring new approaches to community building outside of city government. On the other hand, I cared passionately about the Department of Neighborhoods and the many communities with which we had partnered. I feared that the department's future in city government might not last much longer than my own.

It is now 2006, four years since I wrote the original conclusion. Thankfully, the department and most of its programs and longtime staff are still in place. More than three thousand Neighborhood Matching Fund projects have been completed in those four years, and the number of community gardens has grown to seventy-two. Neighborhood plan implementation continues with the completion of new and improved parks, libraries, community centers, and Neighborhood Service Centers throughout Seattle.

On the other hand, reduced city revenues in 2003 and 2004 hit the department especially hard. The formal Neighborhood Leadership Program was eliminated. About $1.3 million in project money was cut from the Neighborhood Matching Fund. All six sector-manager positions were terminated as the Neighborhood Service Center coordinators were saddled with the additional responsibility of managing neighborhood plan implementation.

Although the cuts reinforce my belief that community organizations should not become dependent on government, they also make me question whether we should have done more to institutionalize the department's programs—specifically, to facilitate the creation of a stronger system of community organizations. "Organizers organize organizations," was Tom Gaudette's mantra. Our approach, however, was to "let a hundred flowers bloom." We believed that encouraging grassroots initiatives was a more appropriate role for government than creating or reinforcing a particular type of organization. Whereas cities with formal citizen participation structures focus on a manageable number of neighborhood associations, Seattle partners with an eclectic assortment of hundreds of community organizations. With the exception of the community councils and neighborhood business associations, however, Seattle's organizations are poorly networked. Because its organizations—which are voluntary and largely unstaffed—have little contact with one another, it is difficult for them to join forces, and separately, it is difficult for any one of them to have an impact on larger issues. Most tend to confine their attention to issues specific to their own community. Consequently, Mayor Nickels was able to get away with disproportionately large cuts to the budget of the Department of Neighborhoods.

Certainly, though, budget cuts to neighborhood programs are not unique to Seattle. The Tufts researchers found that neighborhood associations in cities with formal citizen participation structures are no better equipped to tackle citywide issues. In most instances, although tiered structures formally link neighborhood associations at the district and citywide levels, the connections are more apparent on an organizational chart than they are in reality. As Seattle has learned with its City Neighborhood Council, coordination between the citywide, district, and grassroots levels is inherently challenging. Communication occurs too slowly for effective action to take place.

If there is any hope of bringing together different community interests, the logical place to start is at the local level. Cities with formal citizen participation structures seek to do this by creating representative neighborhood associations. Officially recognized associations are required to conduct extensive outreach in order to be as representative as possible of all residents. City government provides staff support, newsletter assistance, and training to help the neighborhood associations meet this expectation.

There are times when I wonder if a formal, representative structure like this could have been helpful to Seattle's neighborhood planning program. Because there was no one organization that adequately represented all of the constituencies in a given neighborhood, such organizations had to be created before the planning process could begin. Funding to undertake a plan was contingent on neighborhood leaders forming a committee that included all key stakeholders. These committees worked effectively to accomplish their goals. Then, once plans were completed, most participants returned to their own organizations or dropped out entirely, leaving a relatively small group to handle the ongoing advocacy and involvement that are so essential to successful plan implementation. In most neighborhoods, the planning committee disbanded, leaving responsibility for implementation to one or more of the preexisting organizations. Over time, lack of a consistent, ongoing structure has dissipated the advocacy for neighborhood plans. The recent cutbacks in staffing for plan implementation are one result.

Even so, it is not clear that the recognized neighborhood associations in the cities with formal citizen participation structures are any more broadly based than Seattle's community councils. These cities' associations typically lack representation from neighborhood businesses, property owners, and local institutions. Residents with low incomes are underrepresented in the neighborhood associations, according to the Tufts researchers—just as they are in Seattle's community councils. Clearly, there are trade-offs between the relative inclusiveness of Seattle's neighborhood planning committees and the greater permanency of the recognized neighborhood associations in other cities.

Building inclusive, broad-based neighborhood organizations and bringing them together to work effectively at a citywide level are challenges that remain to be addressed—in Seattle and elsewhere. I look forward to reading someone else's book on that topic. Meanwhile, I will cherish Seattle's strong sense of community and the many ways in which organized citizens are contributing so much to our quality of life.

APPENDIX A: MAPS

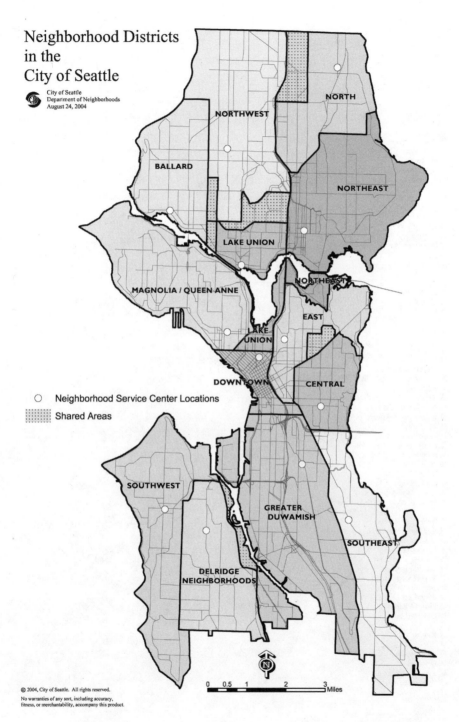

Neighborhood Districts in the City of Seattle

City of Seattle
Department of Neighborhoods
August 24, 2004

○ Neighborhood Service Center Locations

░░░ Shared Areas

NORTH

NORTHWEST

BALLARD

NORTHEAST

LAKE UNION

MAGNOLIA / QUEEN ANNE

NORTHEAST

EAST

LAKE UNION

DOWNTOWN

CENTRAL

SOUTHWEST

GREATER DUWAMISH

SOUTHEAST

DELRIDGE NEIGHBORHOODS

0   0.5   1   2   3 Miles

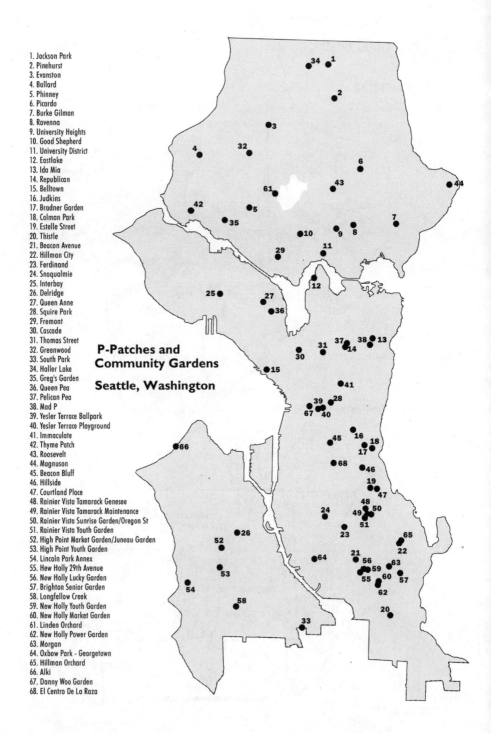

1. Jackson Park
2. Pinehurst
3. Evanston
4. Ballard
5. Phinney
6. Picardo
7. Burke Gilman
8. Ravenna
9. University Heights
10. Good Shepherd
11. University District
12. Eastlake
13. Ida Mia
14. Republican
15. Belltown
16. Judkins
17. Bradner Garden
18. Colman Park
19. Estelle Street
20. Thistle
21. Beacon Avenue
22. Hillman City
23. Ferdinand
24. Snoqualmie
25. Interbay
26. Delridge
27. Queen Anne
28. Squire Park
29. Fremont
30. Cascade
31. Thomas Street
32. Greenwood
33. South Park
34. Haller Lake
35. Greg's Garden
36. Queen Pea
37. Pelican Pea
38. Mad P
39. Yesler Terrace Ballpark
40. Yesler Terrace Playground
41. Immaculate
42. Thyme Patch
43. Roosevelt
44. Magnuson
45. Beacon Bluff
46. Hillside
47. Courtland Place
48. Rainier Vista Tamarack Genesee
49. Rainier Vista Tamarack Maintenance
50. Rainier Vista Sunrise Garden/Oregon St
51. Rainier Vista Youth Garden
52. High Point Market Garden/Juneau Garden
53. High Point Youth Garden
54. Lincoln Park Annex
55. New Holly 29th Avenue
56. New Holly Lucky Garden
57. Brighton Senior Garden
58. Longfellow Creek
59. New Holly Youth Garden
60. New Holly Market Garden
61. Linden Orchard
62. New Holly Power Garden
63. Morgan
64. Oxbow Park - Georgetown
65. Hillman Orchard
66. Alki
67. Danny Woo Garden
68. El Centro De La Raza

**P-Patches and
Community Gardens**

Seattle, Washington

APPENDIX B: NEIGHBORHOOD MATCHING FUND GUIDELINES

Neighborhood Matching Fund
Small and Simple Projects Fund
and Large Projects Fund

http://www.seattle.gov/neighborhoods

What Is the Neighborhood Matching Fund?

The Neighborhood Matching Fund supports local grassroots action in neighborhoods. It is a resource available to neighborhood groups interested in doing projects that address a specific community need *and* that also build community. Neighborhood-based groups can apply for and receive funds to carry out neighborhood-initiated planning, organizing, or improvement projects in partnership with the City of Seattle. Neighborhood Matching Fund dollars are matched by the community's contribution of volunteer labor, donated materials, supplies, services, or cash.

The Two Funds:

Small and Simple Projects Fund	Large Projects Fund
• Applications accepted 4 times a year	• Applications accepted at least once a year
• Applications reviewed by rotating team of Department of Neighborhoods staff	• Applications reviewed by citizens on District Councils and a Citywide Review Team
• Notice of award within 5 weeks	• Notice of award within 3 months
• Awards of up to $15,000	• Awards over $15,000 up to $100,000
• Projects must be completed within six months of contracting	• Projects must be completed within one year of contracting

Who Can Apply?
Applications are accepted from:

• Neighborhood-based organizations of residents or businesses.

• Local, community-based organizations that advocate for the interests of people of color.

• Ad-hoc groups of neighbors who form a committee solely for the purpose of a specific project.

The applicant group must have an open membership and must actively seek involvement from area residents and/or businesses.

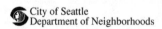

City of Seattle
Department of Neighborhoods

700 3RD AVE STE 400 • SEATTLE WA 98104-1848 • (206) 684-0464

1

j:\NMFforms\Guidelines\87374.pdf
Revised January 2003

Neighborhood Matching Fund
Small and Simple Projects Fund
and Large Projects Fund

http://www.seattle.gov/neighborhoods

Awards are NOT made to:

- Individual persons or individual businesses.

- Religious organizations, government agencies, political groups, district councils, citywide organizations, universities, hospitals, newspapers, non-local organizations.

- Applicants who have failed to successfully carry out projects funded in the two preceding years.

What Kinds of Projects Are Funded?
To be considered for funding, a project must:
- Provide a public benefit, resulting in a product that benefits a neighborhood.

- Emphasize neighborhood self-help; involve neighborhood people in the planning and implementation of the project.

NOT eligible for funding are projects that:
- Duplicate an existing private or public program.

- Provide ongoing services. The Fund cannot pay for ongoing operating budgets.

- Conflict with existing City policy.

Budget items NOT eligible for funding:
- Food. (However, you can use food expenses or donations as match.)

- Out Of City travel expenses.

- Expenditures or financial commitments made before a Neighborhood Matching Fund contract is signed by all parties.

Project Types
1. **Neighborhood Planning and/or Design Project** –

   Produce a plan, design, or report outlining specific actions that will serve as a guide for future action in or changes to your neighborhood.

2. **Neighborhood Organizing Project** – Create, diversify, or enlarge the membership of a multi-issue neighborhood organization in a low-income neighborhood.

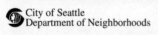

City of Seattle
Department of Neighborhoods

700 3RD AVE STE 400 • SEATTLE WA 98104-1848 • (206) 684-0464

j:\NMFforms\Guidelines\87374.pdf
Revised January 2003

2

3. **Neighborhood Physical Improvement Project** – Build or enhance a physical improvement in your neighborhood.

4. **Neighborhood Non-Physical Improvement Project** – A community building activity or event such as a festival or celebration, a training session, an educational campaign, a computer literacy pilot program, or a workshop. A festival or celebration will only be funded one time. However, if a new community building component is proposed as part of the festival or celebration, then an award for the new component will be given consideration.

5. **Public School Partnership Project** – Pilot or start-up program that directly benefits a public school and the immediate neighborhood.

How Will Your Application Be Reviewed?

Neighborhood Matching Fund applications are reviewed in the following manner:

Small and Simple Projects Fund

- Applications are read and rated by a rotating team of Department of Neighborhoods staff (at least 3 members)

- A team presents its funding recommendations to Department of Neighborhoods management staff.

- Final award decisions are made by the Department director.

Large Projects Fund

- Applications are read and rated by two citizen bodies, the District Council and a Citywide Review Team. District councils only read/ rate projects from their district; the Citywide Review Team reviews and rates all applications.

- District Council and Citywide Review Team ratings are averaged to arrive at an application's "final score."

- The Citywide Review Team prepares award recommendations which are forwarded to the Major and City Council for final approval.

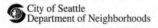

City of Seattle
Department of Neighborhoods

700 3RD AVE STE 400 • SEATTLE WA 98104-1848 • (206) 684-0464

3

j:\NMFforms\Guidelines\87374.pdf
Revised January 2003

Neighborhood Matching Fund
Small and Simple Projects Fund
and Large Projects Fund

http://www.seattle.gov/neighborhoods

How Will Your Application be Rated?

All Neighborhood Matching Fund applications are rated using the following criteria. As you plan your project and write your application, keep these criteria in mind and be sure the application addresses each of them.

Community Benefit

1. Project proposes a good approach to a neighborhood problem; it addresses a clear and pressing need.

   (0 to 10 points)

2. Project activities "build community"; i.e. create stronger bonds between neighbors and greater connections in the community.

   (0 to 15 points)

Participation

1. Project includes opportunities to involve neighbors in shaping and carrying out the project.

   (0 to 10 points)

2. Project promotes interaction of diverse parts of the community (e.g., renters/

   owners, business/residents, intergenerational pairings, different abilities, or different racial and ethnic groups.)

   (0 to 15 points)

Project Feasibility

1. Proposed project is well planned and ready for implementation.

   (0 to 15 points)

2. Budget reliably represents the project's expenses and revenue.

   (0 to 10 points)

Match

1. Match is realistic and appropriate to the project.

   (0 to 15 points)

2. Neighborhood match is documented.

   (0 to 10 points)

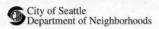

City of Seattle
Department of Neighborhoods

700 3RD AVE STE 400 • SEATTLE WA 98104-1848 • (206) 684-0464

4

j:\NMFforms\Guidelines\87374.pdf
Revised January 2003

Neighborhood Matching Fund
Small and Simple Projects Fund
and Large Projects Fund

http://www.seattle.gov/neighborhoods

Match Requirements

For every dollar requested from the City, the community must provide at least a dollar of match, in the form of cash, donated professional services or materials, or volunteer labor. Applicants should be sure to keep records of all match expended. ***Documenting match is very important and match pledge forms should be submitted with the application.***

Following are requirements for eligible match.

- The total value of the match must equal or exceed the dollar amount requested from the Neighborhood Matching Fund. There are two exceptions: planning projects including design, and neighborhood organizing projects require match that equals or exceeds half the dollar amount requested from the Fund.

- The amount and type of match must be appropriate to the needs of the proposed project. The applicant must be prepared to justify that each element of the match, in the amount proposed, is required to complete the proposed project.

- At least 25% of the neighborhood's match must come from the neighborhood itself rather than from foundations, the County, School District, State, or other entities.

- All volunteer labor is valued at $12 an hour.

- Professional services are valued at the reasonable and customary retail value of the product or service.

- Projects may start counting match as soon as the application is submitted and, if an award is made, continue documenting expended match throughout the contract period. All match must be directly related to planning and implementation of the project.

- Physical design planning may count toward match although it is often expended before the awarded project is implemented. Community volunteer time directly related to developing the design can be counted toward match if it is generated in the six month period prior to the application deadline and is documented with volunteer timesheets.

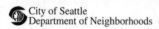

City of Seattle
Department of Neighborhoods

700 3RD AVE STE 400 • SEATTLE WA 98104-1848 • (206) 684-0464

j:\NMFforms\Guidelines\87374.pdf
Revised January 2003

5

Neighborhood Matching Fund
Small and Simple Projects Fund
and Large Projects Fund

http://www.seattle.gov/neighborhoods

- Volunteer time spent on fundraising for a Large Projects Fund project may count as match, but only when it occurs during the six months following the final application date to the Large Projects Fund. This volunteer fundraising time can include grant writing, direct fundraising appeals to individuals, or donated services such as printing and graphics for a fundraising brochure. Neighborhood fundraising time is valued at $12 an hour, even if the volunteer is a professional fundraiser.

- Funds from other City of Seattle sources cannot be counted as match. City of Seattle Community Development Block Grant (CDBG), Pro-Parks, and Community Center levy funds, as well as City staff services, are included in this prohibition.

Match Tips

The best way to start thinking about match is to list all the resources needed to complete the project and then identify which items can be found in the neighborhood. **Documenting match is a very important part of the application.**

Volunteer labor is the resource most readily gained by neighborhood organizations. However, securing volunteer pledges can be time-consuming. It is important to make this investment early in your project so that you can rely on those volunteers as your project moves forward.

Volunteer pledge sheets, either in the form of a log signed by many future volunteers or individual pledge forms, should list each donor's name, the number of hours pledged, address and phone, and the type of job they will do. All pledge sheets should be attached to the application. Volunteer hours pledged to fundraising should specify tasks to be accomplished and those tasks should relate to items included in the project's fundraising plan.

Early on in developing a project, the applicant should discuss potential volunteer activities with the property owner. A property owner may require some elements of the work to be completed by skilled professionals.

Volunteer time spent planning and putting together the application to the

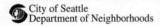

City of Seattle
Department of Neighborhoods

700 3RD AVE STE 400 • SEATTLE WA 98104-1848 • (206) 684-0464

6

j:\NMFforms\Guidelines\87374.pdf
Revised January 2003

http://www.seattle.gov/neighborhoods

Neighborhood Matching Fund or the presentations before the review teams is NOT eligible as match. The one exception to this rule is an allowance for reimbursing up to 10 hours of application preparation time for a Small and Simple Projects Fund application.

Professional services can be an important part of the match so long as the services provided are necessary to the project and valued in proportion to the needs of the project. Applicants should decide early on whether professional services will be donated or paid for with the award. An individual who will be paid for services cannot also pledge volunteer time to be budgeted as match.

The donors of professional services must document the hourly value of their services on professional letterhead. The Neighborhood Matching Fund will recognize the value of professional services at their customary rates.

Donated materials or supplies are valued at their retail price. Borrowed equipment can also be considered as part of the match and valued at the standard rental fee. Here as well, the donor must provide documentation of the value and quantity of the match.

Cash is probably the easiest match to use and to document. An organization that plans to raise cash match should attach a detailed fundraising plan with the application. The fundraising plan should specify fundraising activities, including how much money is expected from each activity, when each activity will occur, and which grantmakers will be applied to. The fundraising plan should demonstrate to reviewers that the applicant has planned and will manage this aspect of the project so as to raise adequate funds within the six months after the application is submitted.

Cash donations may be secured with a written pledge signed by the donor rather than collecting the cash up front.

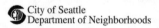

City of Seattle
Department of Neighborhoods

700 3RD AVE STE 400 • SEATTLE WA 98104-1848 • (206) 684-0464

j:\NMFforms\Guidelines\87374.pdf
Revised January 2003

7

Neighborhood Matching Fund
Small and Simple Projects Fund
and Large Projects Fund

http://www.seattle.gov/neighborhoods

Some Points about Public Funding

If your project receives a Neighborhood Matching Fund award, you will encounter certain conditions that are attendant on public funding. Knowing a little about those conditions now will help you plan your budget and your timeline.

Contracts: Award recipients get their money by means of a written contract between the applicant group and the City. There may also be a third party: the organization's fiscal sponsor (see explanation below). This contract explains the terms and methods of getting the money, based on the budget and workplan you propose in your application. In every case, the money is provided to you in installments: as you incur costs, you bill us for the money; we send a check for the amount you claim; then you pay all your vendors.

You cannot begin to incur costs to be paid by the Neighborhood Matching Fund before having a contract with the Department of Neighborhoods.

Included with the invoice you send, you report to us on the match you have expended and on the project's progress. This recordkeeping is key to the project. Even if you have a fiscal sponsor handling the money, your group will have plenty of other project management records to keep. (If a volunteer handles this, remember to consider that recordkeeping as a match item.) Figure three to ten hours a month depending on how big your project is and how much of the work is done by your fiscal sponsor.

Fiscal Sponsor: Handling money, bookkeeping, and bill paying is easy for some and a nightmare for others. It is your choice whether to use a fiscal sponsor: the City does not require you to use another organization. But, especially if your organization does not have experience handling as much money as your project involves, you should carefully consider the advisability of using a fiscal sponsor. If you decide early in your planning process to use a fiscal sponsor, you can budget for that expense. Typically, fiscal sponsors charge as their fee 3% to 10% of the money they handle.

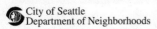

City of Seattle
Department of Neighborhoods

700 3RD AVE STE 400 • SEATTLE WA 98104-1848 • (206) 684-0464

8

j:\NMFForms\Guidelines\87374.pdf
Revised January 2003

Neighborhood Matching Fund
Small and Simple Projects Fund
and Large Projects Fund

An organization does not need 501(c)3 status — that is, an IRS-recognized private, nonprofit charitable organization— to receive City funding. However, donors cannot claim tax benefit for their donations to you unless you are, or are affiliated with, a 501(c) 3. Foundations can make gifts only to 501(c) 3 organizations. Becoming a 501(c) 3 requires an IRS filing process, a fee, and a long wait, maybe a year, before you get your determination.

It isn't difficult to find a fiscal sponsor for your project's award: it can be a community-based nonprofit, a small or large business, or virtually anyone reliable and able and willing to monitor your progress and to report to the IRS at the end of the year for you on the disposition of funds. The Department of Neighborhoods can suggest organizations that have effectively served this function for other groups. It makes sense to choose an IRS-recognized nonprofit 501(c)3 as your fiscal sponsor if you plan to do significant fundraising.

The fiscal sponsor usually handles only the cash and not other kinds of donations to your project. You will still be held responsible for tracking and reporting on volunteer time and other donations. If you keep track of the donations effectively, the fiscal sponsor will have an easy time invoicing the City. The fiscal sponsor will probably want to be assured of your abilities to keep up your end of the deal.

If you want to be your own fiscal sponsor, the Department of Neighborhoods can help you set up simple recordkeeping systems and acquire an IRS Employer Identification Number. You will need to bill the City promptly to keep up your cash flow. You will need to make annual reports to the IRS about disposition of the money you have received. If you hire staff rather than consultants, you will need to operate a payroll and pay payroll taxes.

Insurance: If your project is funded, the City will provide insurance to cover the volunteers while they are at work on your project. However, you will be asked to purchase Commercial General Liability insurance for your project if there is considered to be risk, to limit the liability of your organization as well as the City. Depending on the project's scope and your organization's experience in purchasing insurance, you can expect the price to range from $300 to $1,000.

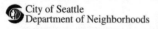

City of Seattle
Department of Neighborhoods

700 3RD AVE STE 400 • SEATTLE WA 98104-1848 • (206) 684-0464

9

j:\NMFforms\Guidelines\87374.pdf
Revised January 2003

Competitive Bid: The City is concerned that you give ample opportunity to a broad set of businesses to bid on the work you are generating. The City encourages opening that opportunity to women- and minority-owned businesses. It is important that you keep an open mind about which stores you purchase from and which consultants and contractors you hire. If you wish to secure consultant services, you must solicit at least three responses to a written scope of work. If the consultant is to receive more than $10,000 of City Funds, you must advertise for those services. Vendor or contractor services (such as printing, or construction work) of over $5,000 must also be secured through an advertised, competitive process.

Contingency: All construction projects must include a contingency allowance in their budgets equaling 15% of all capital expenditures. If you hit any unexpected problems, and chances are you will, you will have some fallback money, but there will be no other funding from the City to address cost overruns.

Steps in Developing a Project

1. Select a Project in Conjunction with the Neighborhood and Build Neighborhood Support.

Choose a project that will generate as much community support as possible and that addresses a known problem or concern. Talk about the project with neighbors and with neighborhood organizations to build as much local support as possible. That support is crucial to the success of your application and your project.

2. Gain Site Control and City Advice.

If your project involves use of or changes to property that your organization does not own, you must get written permission from the owner, e.g., Seattle School District, Seattle Parks and Recreation, Seattle Department of Transportation, or private property owner. Contact Neighborhood Matching Fund staff to get help developing your project idea and application:

3. Develop the Project's Scope.

Begin your work plan with simple goals and objectives. List the activities needed to

---

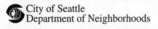

City of Seattle
Department of Neighborhoods

700 3RD AVE STE 400 • SEATTLE WA 98104-1848 • (206) 684-0464

J:\NMF forms\Guidelines\87374.pdf
Revised January 2003

10

accomplish your goals. Some initial research may be needed at this stage to get a handle on the steps involved. You may be able to consult with another neighborhood group that has done a similar project. Do any members of your group have professional experience that could be helpful? Does someone at the City know about this kind of project?

4. Determine Resources Needed.

Resources you will probably need include expertise, equipment, supplies, postage, volunteers and services. You may also need liability insurance, permit fees, maps and technical studies, fiscal sponsor fees, construction management, and information about competitive bidding requirements. If you expect a City department to participate in your project by providing a service, be aware that there may be costs associated with that service. Your list will become a first draft of the detailed budget required in the Neighborhood Matching Fund application.

5. Develop a Project Budget.

After you list needed resources, you will need to estimate costs in order to do a budget. To ensure greater accuracy in your budget, get cost estimates for each budget item from more than one reliable source. Keep careful notes of all conversations with vendors or contractors which involve estimates. Those notes will be helpful to you later when you select contractors.

6. Determine the Match.

See "Match Requirements," pages 3-5.

7. Research Regulations.

Many projects need permits, insurance, or design review before proceeding. Find out what regulations and permits apply to your project.

8. And keep in mind these suggestions to help you submit a competitive application...

- Review all application requirements before you start. Contact Neighborhood

---

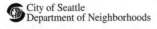

City of Seattle
Department of Neighborhoods

700 3RD AVE STE 400 • SEATTLE WA 98104-1848 • (206) 684-0464

j:\NMFforms\Guidelines\87374.pdf
Revised January 2003

GUIDELINES

Matching Fund staff: they can help make sure your application is competitive and complete.

- Plan for community participation before you develop the application. This will build support for your project and may avoid problems later on in the process.

- Create a timeline, starting with the application's due date and working backward. Allow adequate time to publicize community participation events.

- You must use the budget forms provided in the application or replicate them exactly. You may ask for the application form in a digital format (or download it from: www.seattle.gov/neighborhoods on the Web. However, only printed-out paper copies with attachments and original signature will be accepted.

- Do not assume that reviewers are familiar with your community. Back up what you write with documentation and relevant data. Clearly describe the public benefit and neighborhood participation process used to develop your proposal.

- To have an effective project and a competitive application, neighborhood participation should involve a broad range of citizens, including representatives from many sectors of the neighborhood. Your application should clearly show how your project is encouraging broad-based participation that results in "building community."

- Consider maintenance for any types of capital improvement project. Who will water the garden, weed the planting, take care of cleaning a mural that gets graffittied, etc. Most types of capital projects require a written maintenance plan developed by the community and in consultation with the property owner. Further, if a project results in increased maintenance costs, your organization and the property owner should decide how those costs will be covered.

- A complete application includes: any necessary attachments in 8½ x 11 format; and an original application and required copies signed by the chair of the organization. Late applications will not be accepted.

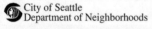

City of Seattle
Department of Neighborhoods

700 3RD AVE STE 400 • SEATTLE WA 98104-1848 • (206) 684-0464

12

j:\NMFforms\Guidelines\87374.pdf
Revised January 2003

BIBLIOGRAPHY

Alinsky, Saul D. *Reveille for Radicals*. New York: Vintage Books, 1946.

———. *Rules for Radicals*. New York: Vintage Books, 1972.

Berry, Jeffrey M., Kent E. Portney, and Ken Thomson. *The Rebirth of Urban Democracy*. Washington, D.C.: The Brookings Institution, 1993.

Boyte, Harry C. *Commonwealth: A Return to Citizen Politics*. New York: The Free Press, 1989.

Kemmis, Daniel. *Community and the Politics of Place*. Norman: University of Oklahoma Press, 1990.

King, Cheryl Simrell, and Camilla Stivers. *Government Is Us: Public Administration in an Anti-Government Era*. Thousand Oaks: SAGE Publications, 1998.

Klinenberg, Eric. *Heat Wave: A Social Autopsy of Disaster in Chicago*. Chicago: University of Chicago Press, 2002.

Kretzmann, John P., and John L. McKnight. *Building Communities from the Inside Out: A Path Toward Finding and Mobilizing a Community's Assets*. Evanston: Institute for Policy Research, Northwestern University, 1993.

Lappé, Frances Moore, and Paul Martin DuBois. *The Quickening of America: Rebuilding Our Nation, Remaking Our Lives*. San Francisco: Jossey-Bass, 1994.

Loeb, Paul Rogat. *Soul of a Citizen: Living with Conviction in a Cynical Time*. New York: St. Martin's, Griffin, 1999.

Mattessich, Paul, and Barbara Monsey. *Community Building: What Makes It Work*. St. Paul: Amherst H. Wilder Foundation, 1997.

McKnight, John. *The Careless Society: Community and Its Counterfeits*. New York: Basic Books, 1995.

McLean, Scott L., David A. Schultz, and Manfred B. Steger. *Social Capital: Critical Perspectives on Community and "Bowling Alone."* New York: New York University Press, 2002.

Medoff, Peter, and Holly Sklar. *Streets of Hope: The Fall and Rise of an Urban Neighborhood*. Boston: South End Press, 1994.

Osborne, David, and Ted Gaebler. *Reinventing Government: How the Entrepreneurial Spirit Is Transforming the Public Sector.* Reading, Mass.: Addison-Wesley, 1992.

Putnam, Robert D. *Bowling Alone: The Collapse and Revival of American Community.* New York: Touchstone, 2000.

Putnam, Robert D., and Lewis M. Feldstein. *Better Together: Restoring the American Community.* New York: Simon and Schuster, 2003.

Sirianni, Carmen, and Lewis Friedland. *Civic Innovation in America: Community Empowerment, Public Policy, and the Movement for Civic Renewal.* Berkeley: University of California Press, 2001.

Thomson, Ken. *From Neighborhood to Nation: The Democratic Foundations of Civil Society.* Hanover: Tufts University Press, 2001.

Warren, Mark R. *Dry Bones Rattling: Community Building to Revitalize American Democracy.* Princeton: Princeton University Press, 2001.

INDEX

ACORN (Association of Community Organizations for Reform Now), 11

Adcock, Joe, 37

alienation and apathy, 18

Alinsky, Saul, 23; and Back of the Yards Neighborhood Council, 8–9; and Ernesto Cortes, 10; and Tom Gaudette, 16; and John McKnight, 14, 41; organizing principles of, 8; and Robert Putnam, 8; *Reveille for Radicals*, 8; *Rules for Radicals*, 8, 14

Angeles, Ron, 148

artistic creations, 75, 116–17; in Belltown P-Patch, 113–14; in Bradner Gardens Park, 123–25; in Carkeek Park, 97–98; dragon poles, 57; mosaics in Orca garden, 150–51; murals, 56, 72–76, 158–59; Ron Bills Fountain, 58; Sadako sculpture, 79; totem in Baker Park, 90; in Weather Watch Park, 80; in Webster Park, 89; whale fin sculpture in Columbia City, 154. See also *Beckoning Cistern*; Fremont Troll

asset-based community development, 13–15, 16, 41

Asset-Based Community Development Institute, 16, 41

Badanes, Steve, 71, 127

Baker Park, 89–90

Balch, Ginger, 39–40

Balch, Raymond, 39–40

ball field renovation: Meadowbrook, 93–94; Rainier, 150

Baltimore, 163

Barker, John, 96

Beatwalk, 156

Beckoning Cistern, 116–17

Bellevue, Washington, 162

Belltown Cottages, 115

Belltown P-Patch, 112–15

Bercuvitz, Jeff, 41–42

Bike Works, 152–53

Birmingham, Alabama, 11–12, 16

block watch, 6, 21, 35, 45, 172

boatbuilding by kids, 92–93

Bockmann, Dave, 33

Boston, 15, 44

Bowling Alone (Putnam), 3–4, 8; critique of, 5–7

Boyd, Dave, 89

Boyte, Harry, 8

Bradner Gardens Park, 121–25

Broeske, Ellen, 148
Buffalo, New York, 163
Building Communities from the Inside Out (Kretzmann and McKnight), 14
building renovations: Belltown Cottages, 115; Bike Works storefront, 153; Bradner Gardens Park, 124–25; Eritrean Community Center, 99; Rainier Valley Cultural Center, 153–54

Campbell, Linda, 168–69
Cano, Lupita, 37
Capitol Hill Neighborhood Plan, 38, 51
Carkeek Park salmon playground, 96–98
Carlson, Carolyn, 35–37
Cascade P-Patch, 117–18
Charlotte, North Carolina, 166
Chepe, Eugenio Fuster, 125–27
Chicago, 4, 8–9, 14
Chief Seattle Social Club, 127
Chong, Charlie, 76–77
City Neighborhood Council (Seattle), 53; communication challenges of, 174; and Neighborhood Matching Fund, 59–60, 62, 63, 70, 128
civic engagement: benefits of, 19–20; citizen participation versus community empowerment, 20–21, 31–32; government's role in, 172–73; in Seattle, 5–6, 19
Civic Innovation in America (Sirianni and Friedland), 13
civil rights. *See* Office of Civil Rights
Cleveland, Ohio, 163
College Street Ravine, 56, 76–77
Columbia City: Beatwalk in, 156;
Bike Works in, 152–53; farmers market in, 156–57; history of, 147; landmark district of, 148; Neighborhood Service Center in, 46; Orca community garden in, 150; pornographic theater in, 20, 148, 164; Powerful Schools in, 151–52; Rainier Community Center in, 149–50; storefront murals in, 158–59; town meetings in, 155–59
Columbus, Ohio, 162, 166
communities of color: and African American oral history, 91–92; and Eritrean Community Center, 99–100; and ethnic festivals, 141; and expropriation of buildings, 6; and Hillside Garden, 110–12; and Horn of Africa Computer Center, 154–55; mutual assistance associations for, 33; and Neighborhood Matching Fund eligibility, 60–61
community councils. *See* neighborhood associations
community, defined, 170
community gardens. *See* P-Patch Program
community organizing, 8–11; Department of Neighborhoods' role in, 33–35; techniques of, 25–26, 41, 42, 170–71
community schools, 20, 56, 151–52, 172
community visioning, 13
composting, 118–21
Comprehensive Plan of Seattle, 105, 131–36, 159
computer centers: and Grassroots Technology Center, 152; and

Horn of Africa Computer Center,
154–55; and Project Compute,
149
Conlin, Richard, 63, 121, 136, 138
Constantine, Blair and Dow, 77
Construction and Land Use, Department of, 106
COPS (Communities Organized for
Public Service), 9–11
Cortes, Ernesto, 9–10
Courtland P-Patch, 106–8
Coyote Junior High, 74–75, 123–24
crime prevention, 45, 83–85, 172.
See also block watch
Cronander, Cheryl, 155
Cruzen, Earl, 72–73

Daubert, Karen, 81–82
Dayton, Ohio, 11–13, 16
Department of Neighborhoods
(Seattle). *See* Neighborhoods,
Department of
Detroit, 163
developmental disabilities, 19, 35;
definition of, 35–36; involving
people with, 36–40
Diers, Jim: and arrival in Seattle, 21–
22; and Belltown P-Patch, 114;
and Carkeek Park, 96; and Columbia City, 150; and Cuba, 125–27;
and district councils, 51, 53–54;
employment history of, 16; firing
of, 168–69; and *Fremont Troll*, 69–
70; and Group Health Cooperative, 26–27; and Hillside Garden,
11; and Interbay P-Patch, 121;
and Involving All Neighbors, 35–
39; and Lake City Community
Council, 34; and Neighbor Appreciation Day, 142–46; and Neigh-

borhood Matching Fund, 56; and
neighborhood planning, 128, 132;
and Operation Homestead, 85;
and replication of neighborhood
programs, 161–62; and SESCO,
23–25
district councils: in Birmingham,
Dayton, Portland, St. Paul, 11–13;
in Seattle, 29, 48–54, 59, 130, 149
Drago, Jan, 52
dragon poles, 57
Driggs, Sarah, 21, 149
Dry Bones Rattling (Warren), 10–11
Dudley Street Neighborhood Initiative (DSNI), 7, 15
Duluth, Minnesota, 166

Empire-Kenyon crosswalk issue,
23–24
Eritrean Community Center, 99–100
Eugene, Oregon, 163
Everett, Washington, 162

farmers markets, 5, 35; in Columbia
City, 156–57
formal citizen participation structures, 11–13
Fremont Time, 36–37
Fremont Troll, 56, 69–71, 127
Friends of P-Patch, 102, 104, 106

Galluzzo, Greg, 16
Gamaliel Foundation, 10, 16
Garfield Drug-Free Zone, 56, 83–85
Gaudette, Tom, 16, 26, 173
gay and lesbian community, 6, 51,
65, 153
Geise, Carolyn, 115–16
Ghebremedhin, Asmellash, 100
Government Is Us (King and Stivers), 13

governments' dual dilemma, 18

Gowan, Dervilla, 87

gray to green, 56, 89, 150–51

Green, Pamela, 148

Grinnell, Iowa, 21, 22

Groundswell Northwest, 88–91

Group Health Cooperative, 26

Growing Vine Street, 115–17

Growth Management Act (Washington), 131

Hackett, Regina, 70–71

Harmon, Susan, 39–40

Havana, 125–27

Heart of Phinney, 82–83

Helping Link, 33

Hillside Garden, 110–12

Historic Preservation Program, 30, 148

homeless people: art gallery for, 87; and Garden of Homeless Angels, 43; and Operation Homestead, 85–86; outreach van for, 86; voucher program for, 87

Horn of Africa Computer Center, 154–55

housing. *See* Office of Housing (Seattle); Seattle Housing Authority

Houston, 163

IAF (Industrial Areas Foundation), 9–10

Information Technology, Seattle Department of, 167

Interbay P-Patch, 118–21

Involving All Neighbors, 35–40

Iraq invasion, neighborhood-based opposition to, 6

"iron rule" of organizing, 10, 14

Jane, Lezlie, 81

Jefferson Parish, Louisiana, 163

Joncas, Kate, 52–53

Kemmis, Daniel, *Community and the Politics of Place*, 4–5, 172

King, Cheryl Simrell, *Government Is Us*, 13

King County, Seattle, 106, 131, 167

Kinney, Karen, 156

Klinenberg, Eric, *Heat Wave*, 4

Kretzmann, John (Jody), 16, 41; *Building Communities from the Inside Out*, 14

Lake Forest Park, Washington, 162

Lantana, Florida, 166

Lappé, Frances Moore, *The Quickening of America*, 13, 14

Las Vegas, 163

lessons learned, 169–73

libraries, 139–40, 160; with Neighborhood Service Centers, 35, 44, 137

Little City Halls. *See* Neighborhood Service Centers

Los Angeles, 166

Lucile Street Bridge, 25

McDade, Charles, 145

McDermott, Kate, 119

McKnight, John, 13, 16, 40–41; *Building Communities from the Inside Out*, 14–15; *The Careless Society*, 14

McLean, Vivian, 53–54

Madison, Wisconsin, 163

Malmgren, Nancy, 96

Matsuno, Bernie, 60

Meadowbrook Wetlands, 93–94

Medoff, Peter, and Holly Sklar, *Streets of Hope*, 7, 15
Merki, Lisa, 94
Moss, Larry, 38–39
Moty, Joyce, 126–27
Murals of West Seattle, 72–73

Nante, France, 163
Neighbor Appreciation Day, 142–46
neighborhood associations: benefits to government, 32; in Birmingham, Dayton, Portland, 11–13; officially recognized versus independent, 12–13, 32, 61, 173–75; in Seattle, 22–23, 33, 50–51; variety of, 34
Neighborhood Leadership Program, 31, 35
Neighborhood Matching Fund, 46, 101–2; benefits of, 57–59, 171; budget cuts to, 173–74; citizen review process for, 59–60; and Citywide Review Team, 59, 63, 64; contracts for, 67; eligibility and selection criteria for, 60–62; fiscal sponsors for, 67; funding sources for, 67; growth of, 62–65; *Help Yourself!* booklets on, 68; Ideas Fair for, 68; Innovations Award to, 55–56; innovative projects of, 56; Large Projects Fund of, 64; low-income communities eligibility for, 62; match requirements for, 60–61; for neighborhood planning, 128–33, 140; origin of, 29; in other cities, 163, 166; other departments involved with, 56–57; Outreach Fund of, 65; project types eligible for, 55; projects funded by, 69–100, 106–

25, 142, 148–59; public school partnerships with, 61; Small and Simple Projects Fund of, 63–64; Tree Fund of, 65–66; workshops for, 68; Youth Fund of, 65
neighborhood planning, 128–140; benefits of, 171; budget cuts to, 173; in Columbia City, 149, 159–60; and NIMBYism, 165; origin of, 29
Neighborhood Planning and Assistance Program, 29–30, 48, 49, 52
Neighborhood Planning Office, 30, 133–134, 138, 159
Neighborhood Rights Campaign, 132
Neighborhood Service Centers, 35, 137, 140, 144, 148; coordinators of, 27–48, 50, 142, 148–49, 154; history of, 29–30, 44; locations of, 44; in other cities, 162, 163; services offered by, 44–47
Neighborhoods, Department of: growth of, 21, 30; mission of, 21, 30; origin of, 28–30
Neighborhoods, of Seattle, 22–23: Admiral, 76–77; Alki, 56, 80–81, 98; Ballard, 28, 74, 87, 88, 92, 136; Beacon Hill, 23, 43, 131; Belltown, 74, 112–17; Broadview, 96–98; Capitol Hill, 38, 43, 51, 87; Cascade, 56, 117–18, Central Area, 33, 56, 72, 91–92, 98; Columbia City, 20, 46, 147–160; Courtland Place, 106–8; Crown Hill, 89–91; Delridge, 39, 43, 53–54; Denny Regrade, 52, 87; Downtown, 52–53, 85–86; Dunlap, 94; Eastlake, 98; Floating Homes, 92–93; Fremont, 28, 36–37, 56, 69–71, 74;

Neighborhoods, of Seattle *(continued)*
Garfield, 56, 83–85; Georgetown,
23, 164; Green Lake, 74; Hillman
City, 63; Holly Park, 24; International District, 52, 57, 74, 131;
Judkins Park, 74; Lake City, 34–
35; Laurelhurst, 145–46, Leschi,
81–82; Madison Valley, 78–79,
145; Madrona, 77–78, 144; Magnolia, 43; Meadowbrook, 93–94;
Miller Park, 58; Mount Baker, 34,
110–12, 151; Phinney Ridge, 82–
83, 108–10, 142; Pike-Pine, 131,
137; Pioneer Square, 52, 86–87;
Pritchard Beach, 94–95; Queen
Anne, 131, 146; Rainier Valley, 23,
33, 99, 106–8, 154; Rainier Vista,
63; Ravenna, 39; Roosevelt, 131;
Seward Park, 66; SODO, 73–74;
South Park, 74, 92; Sunset Hill,
88–89; University District, 43, 47,
137; Uptown, 137; Wallingford,
22, 136; Wedgwood, 43; West
Seattle, 39, 40, 53–54, 72–73;
Westwood, 39
Nickels, Greg, 121, 168, 173
NIMBY (Not In My Back Yard),
163–65
North Rainier Neighborhood Plan,
110

Office of Civil Rights (Seattle), 45
Office of Housing (Seattle), 45
Operation Homestead, 85–86
oral histories, 91–92
Orca garden, 150–51
Owens, Garry, 33

Pacific Hotel, 85–86
park development, 35, 39–40; through

Neighborhood Matching Fund,
79–83, 88–91, 121–25; through
neighborhood planning, 136–37,
140
Parks and Recreation, Department
of: and Neighborhood Matching
Fund, 56–57, 65, 68, 88, 93–94,
167; and P-Patch Program, 106,
115, 121–22
Pate, Makeeba, 92
Penalosa, Enrique, 162
People First, 40
Peringer, Mike, 73–74
Phinney Ridge P-Patch, 108–10
PICO (Pacific Institute for Community Organization), 10
Planning Commission, 29–30
playground construction, 56, 96–98;
workshops on, 67–68
police. *See* Seattle Police Department
Port Elizabeth, South Africa, 163
Portland, Oregon, 11–12, 16, 29, 161,
167
Powerful Schools, 56, 151–52
P-Patch Program: benefits of, 102–
3; community gatherings in,
142; expansion plans of, 105–6;
gardens developed for, 106–25;
meaning of the *P* in, 101; merger
with Department of Neighborhoods, 30; operations of, 101–2;
property ownership of, 106; and
public housing, 104–5
Pritchard Beach Wetlands, 94–95
public restrooms, 52
Putnam, Robert, *Bowling Alone*, 3–8,
17

Quickening of America, The (Lappé
and DuBois), 13

rain harvest projects: Cascade, 117–18; Growing Vine Street, 115–17

Rainier Community Center, 130, 149–50

Rainier Valley Cultural Center, 153–54

Rebirth of Urban Democracy, The (Berry, Portney, and Thomsen), 11, 13, 174–75

reforestation with native plants, 56, 76–79

reinventing government critique, 18

replication of neighborhood programs, 161–67

ReTree Ballard, 87

Reveille for Radicals (Alinsky), 8

Rice, Norm, 30, 34, 69, 85; and neighborhood planning, 132–33, 137; and Neighbor Appreciation Day, 142–43

Riley, Lillian, 88

Ron K. Bills Fountain (Seattle), 58

Rowley, John, 119–21

Royer, Charles, 27, 29, 50

Ruder, Karma, 132–33

Rules for Radicals (Alinsky), 8, 14

Sadinsky, Rebecca, 60

St. Paul, Minnesota, 11–13, 16, 29, 161, 167

St. Petersburg, Florida, 166

Salt Lake City, 163

San Antonio, Texas, 9, 11, 162

San Diego, 163

Santa Monica, 163

Sarasota, Florida, 163

Schell, Paul, 62–63, 137–40, 168–69

Schmoe, Floyd, 79

schools. *See* Seattle School District

Schultz, David, *Social Capital: Critical Perspectives*, 7

Seattle Arts Commission, 57, 70–71

Seattle Center, 120–21

Seattle City Light, 44, 106, 124

Seattle Department of Transportation: and Neighborhood Matching Fund, 56–57, 65, 79, 81, 82, 167; and P-Patch Program, 106–7

Seattle Peace Park, 79

Seattle Police Department, 20, 45, 106, 138

Seattle Post-Intelligencer, 70–71

Seattle Public Utilities, 44, 57, 106, 167

Seattle School District, 20, 106, 148; and Neighborhood Matching Fund, 57, 68, 88

Seattle Times, 85, 100, 143–44

sector strategy, 138–40, 159

SEED (Southeast Effective Development), 130–31, 153–54

Senior Citizens, Mayor's Office of, 45

September 11, 2001: 83, 120–21

SESCO (South End Seattle Community Organization), 23–25, 28, 164

Sher, Ron, 162

Shoreline, Washington, 163

Simpson, Buster, 116

Sirianni, Carmen, *Civic Innovation in America*, 13

Sklar, Holly, and Peter Medoff, *Streets of Hope*, 7, 15

Small Sparks, 41–43

Smith, Darryl, 156

social capital, 4–7

Social Capital: Critical Perspectives (Schultz), 7

SODO urban art corridor, 73–74

Southeast Seattle Action Plan, 129–31, 149, 155

Stewart, George, 83
Strategic Planning Office, 135
Street, Jim, 29, 50
Streets of Hope (Medoff and Sklar), 7, 15
String of Pearls, 81–82
suburban communities, 162
Sussman, Jerry, 79
sustainability, 171

Thomsen, Ken, *Neighborhoods to Nation*, 11–12; *The Rebirth of Urban Democracy,* 11
transportation. *See* Seattle Department of Transportation
tree planting: ReTree Ballard, 87; Tree Fund, 65–66

University of Washington, 68, 118, 122, 127
urban villages, 132, 133

Vancouver, B.C., 166
VanSanden, Janine, 93–94

Victoria, B.C., 163
Vinh, Diana, 106–8

Walsh, Terry, 96
Warren, Mark, *Dry Bones Rattling,* 10–11
Weather Watch Park, 80–81
Webster Park, 88–89
wetlands restoration, 56, 93–95
Whittaker, Matthew, 39
Wichita, 163
Wood, Judith, 142–43

youth programs: African American oral history, 91–92; Bike Works, 152–53; boatbuilding for kids, 92–93; gardens for youth, 43, 103, 105, 150; murals of Garfield, SODO, Medgar Evers, 72–75; Powerful Schools, 151–52; Project Compute, 149; Youth Fund, 65; Youth Theater, 154

Zarker, Gary, 69